Stephen Ellis Hamilton

LETTING GO THE LEASH

Edited by Robin Wollaeger

Oil On Water Press

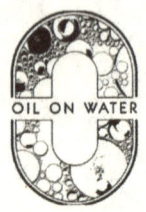

OIL ON WATER PRESS
Oxford, UK
First published in 2022
office@oilonwaterpress.com

LETTING GO THE LEASH

Cover photo : STEPHEN ELLIS HAMILTON
Cover design : MARK CRITCHELL < mark.critchell@gmail.com >
Layout : GANYMEDE FOLEY
The Publisher wishes to thank Leigh Bushell

10 9 8 7 6 5 4 3 2 1

A CIP catalogue record for this book is available from the British Library

ISBN PAPERBACK 978-1-909394-87-2
ISBN E-BOOK 978-1-909394-88-9

ORIGINAL TRUE-LIFE STORIES & MEMOIR

Exclusive content at **OILONWATERPRESS.COM**

Contents

Dedicated to Alex and Anthony

PREFACE

WHILE STANDING IN the street gazing up at four long-stemmed champagne glasses twinkling in the bright morning sun of Saturday, March 4th, 2020 I realized that life for me would never be the same again.

The tall cabinet holding those delicate glasses rose high above me on the second floor of a roofless building. Blown off the night before, the twisted roof was gone, the brick walls bent inward into the ravaged rooms and lay collapsed into a pile of rubble.

Twelve hours prior, an F3 tornado had torn through this historic neighborhood, known as Germantown for the mid-19th century immigrants who settled here in the old Victorian houses on the street where I stood. But the cabinet had been spared, it's four fragile glasses remained standing, waiting for someone to appreciate their inner grit.

I was holding onto a leash, at the end of which was the dog I had rescued four years prior; we had hiked hundreds of miles and had some harrowing adventures, he had witnessed devastation in kill shelters, and from human hands, but this tableau was something new, a devastation he had never seen. He sat silently to my right staring at the same horrible scene, his expression, one of complacency, never changing.

I didn't have time to ponder if he understood that life was as fragile as the glasses and indefensible as the fallen bricks, pulling the dog beside me into a fast clip we continued on through the debris in the street. Having to wait for the tornado to pass we had just hiked the 4 miles from my house and needed to get moving. My son lived in this neighborhood. I needed to make sure he had survived.

That night when the dog and I returned home, both of my sons safe and accounted for, I started a journal. Things needed to be said. I imagined sitting on Granddaddy Edgar's porch telling him about the dog, 9/11, the shifts and turns my life had taken, a possible felony I had mistakenly committed, the tornado, and this new pandemic, to name a few. He had survived the pandemic of 1918, had had a successful marriage, knew the value of a good dog and a sturdy flat-bed truck. I could have used his council.

As the pandemic emptied the streets, I saw my future bottom out and could do little else but stare at the walls, with not much else to do but follow the dog as he took the lead through my silent city by day, I recorded my recollections, conversations, flashbacks, everything I wanted to bring into focus by night. My journal grew into the pages of emotions that became this book.

Of the many stories that will be born out of the challenges faced in the global pandemic of 2020, this one is ours, mine and the dog's.

Without the skill, patience and encouragement of my editor, Robin Wollaeger, this story would not have been possible. In my hours of doubt she gently supported me and told me to keep writing. She cheered me on when I finished chapters and kept me honest to the end. She has my endless thanks for her faith and willingness to see this through to completion, I would not have trusted the manuscript to go to the publisher until she gave me her seal of approval.

This is my first book.

CHAPTER I
THE GIFT

IT WAS THE worst Christmas ever. I had come home from work to find two cars in my front yard and my 'gift' from my oldest son, Alex, quietly sizing up my living room furniture.

Up to this point, Alex had always shown reasonable judgment. Smart, athletic, solid good looks with a trim beard and a heart of gold; in my little family, he is our rock. He is the pragmatist, the peacekeeper of our fragile threesome: his younger brother, Anthony, and me. But this decision had me scratching my head.

How could he think that planting another dog in my life would be something I'd want for Christmas?

And now here I was looking down the barrel at a fifty-some-odd pound rescue who wouldn't even look me in the eye. Black and white with short, coarse fur, a square head sported a crisp, white, wishbone pattern that shaped his face. A scrawny adolescent pup who looked poised to grow into an exceptionally large dog. His long boney tail stood straight out at an angle. It was not wagging. Like a gangster in a 1920s movie, his poker face gave nothing away as his eyes slowly cased the joint for exits.

I am still trim and fit in a banker's suit Monday through Friday with a stock of thick white hair; I have been described as a Steve Martin look-a-like. As a single dad, I had spent the last twenty-five years helping two sons grow to adulthood which will forever stand out as my biggest challenge and greatest pleasure in life. And don't get me wrong, I love animals. Over the course of thirty years, we've owned dogs, cats, lizards, a few fish, a gerbil, several hamsters, and a king snake named Clyde. Most all of them are buried in my backyard, and if some future builder decides to dig up the yard, they will find so many pet bones they'll probably call it in. But at age sixty, I'd been looking forward to beefing up my nest egg, paying off debt, shedding responsibilities, and traveling to exotic places — not being a caretaker for another dog, human, or pet snake for that matter. The next twenty years were supposed to be all about me.

Anthony, younger by a year, with a stout chin and bright almond-shaped eyes, leaned over and chimed in, "Why'd you get dad a dog, Alex?" Our truth-teller, Anthony follows distant drums with a confident swagger; he may meet you in a sharp suit one day and resemble a street urchin the next. With a natural inclination to smile, he, too, was blessed with his mother's good looks. His jet brown wavy hair like a curtain over his eyes as he stared at the mongrel, a smirk on his lips. "He looks funny. Did you find him on the road?"

The boys were quiet again, obviously waiting for my reaction, which was to promptly walk into the kitchen and fix myself a drink. One shot of vodka might help me sort this out. The dog followed me and eyed the back door. I opened it and he loped out, thankfully. I pondered the fact that he might break my flimsy backyard vinyl fence and escape. The thought gave me a grim smile. How was I going to get rid of this dog?

Then it hit me. This mongrel had been the first real adult gift from my son — he had thoughtfully planned it out, spent his own money, shopped for the 'perfect' dog. To see the disappointment on his face, that look of sorrow and dismay that the result of his best efforts to make me happy on Christmas had failed was not an option. Yeah ... I was going to have to keep the dog, oh and yeah, probably buy another damned fence! I fixed another drink (two shots this time). *Merry Christmas!*

I walked outside and looked for the dog. It was night by then; I worried that he'd already escaped through to the alley and turned over a few trash cans for good measure. I saw and heard nothing. I had left him out there too long. I started frantically searching for him, I had nothing to call him by, I did not even know his name, or even if he had one. Then I heard something behind me and turned.

It is difficult to describe the look on this dog's face. I have seen dogs that showed fear, a grimace maybe, some even smile. But this face was unemotional, heartless, detached. I would even say callous. Whatever my feelings were for him, he was letting me know they were mutual. Well, at least we understood each other. Alex walked outside, and then all the hell and fury of a Baskerville hound let loose.

Apparently, one of the neighbor's cats was out for a nightly stroll and got caught in the crosshairs. We all rushed the fence at the same time as the frantic cat tried to protect whatever number of lives it had left.

For ten solid minutes, our neighbors were alerted that not only did I have a dog, but their peace and feline population were very much in jeopardy. After corralling and guiding him to the door, I tried to push him back into the kitchen. He stopped, tensed up, and gave me a low growl and a look that was clear: There would be no pushing this dog in my future. A piece of bread finally did the trick.

It was time for a conversation.

"Dad, he's a rescue." *Oh really? I thought he might be a Westminster Champion. Silly me.*

"Son, what were you thinking? Can't you take him back to the ... whatever?"

"No, dad. He has a chip in him now."

"Well, that's simple. Just extract the chip. Done."

Silence and not the good kind pervaded our tense foursome.

The last dog that I was saddled with was his childhood German Shepherd mix named Girl. Such a sweet name for a dog that regularly liked to bite people. After my ex-wife remarried and moved a state away, there was no way she could keep her. Reluctantly, I had stepped in and offered to save the day, which proved to be quite the challenge since I had just recently adopted two dogs — a lab named Ranger and a cattle dog named Lacy. I ended up newly single with two very young boys and three particularly challenging dogs.

Girl broke out of the yard so many times I had to rig up enough electric livestock fence to make my little house in my clean suburban neighborhood look like a Stalag. Needless to say, I was no longer concerned about robbers, serial killers, or anyone else that wanted to break in. I was concerned about other things like the fact that Lacy, the cattle dog, had decided to challenge Girl for pack leader and was becoming aggressive.

Feeding time was an everyday choreography of balancing and rotating three disagreeable dogs in a tense macho fest. I didn't really have a home as such; I was the operator of a small fight club where I happened to sleep.

I was successful for the better part of a year when things got out of hand. It was on a hot summer day in 2008 that I made the near-fatal mistake of holding the back door open a little too long. Girl and Lacy immediately launched head-to-head in mortal combat. The many months of pent-up frustration resulted in several minutes of fray in the kitchen. Lacy was at the mercy of Girl, who was determined to reduce the number of the three-pack to a two-pack. Before Girl could get in the final neck-breaking lunge, I dove in between them and somehow managed to shove Lacy into the utility room and close the door. I stayed inside for a few minutes to catch my breath while Lacy licked her wounds, and I checked her over for any major cuts.

My hand really hurt, and I needed to get it dressed. Girl, positioned on the other side of the door, had only one thing on her mind, and that was an opportunity to finish the kill. I squeezed the door open and saw that the kitchen was a bloody mess. I managed to slip out of the closet and get Girl out the back door. I needed to nurse Lacy, still in the utility room; she had lost her right upper canine. I knew because it was dug into my right hand. I wondered if it could be put back in her jaw. Probably not.

That night, when it was Girl's turn to sleep inside, Lacy and Ranger disappeared from the backyard. For days, weeks, I followed up with every shelter around and put fliers on telephone poles. No luck. To this day, I do not know what happened to them. It was heartbreaking for all of us. That is, all of us except for Girl. She was real ok with it.

Over the years, Girl became close to me and mellowed with age. No longer interested in breaking out of the yard, she became very protective of it and guarded the fence 24/7. I was finally able to dismantle the Stalag, much to the relief of the neighbors, and she stuck by my side like Velcro.

When the boys were with me, we all piled on the couch where Girl was happiest only if she were within arm's reach of me by a bit of tail or paw. I think that people are complicated and hard to figure — not so with dogs. Being a mixed-breed rescue, Girl had fought her whole life for dominance and acceptance. Now that she had it, she had finally won, was finally 'home.' The boys and I were her ultimate prize, won by her in a death match, owned by her by default. We were her family, and she, the sentinel, the defender, the watchdog head honcho.

When Girl got older, I was finally able to take her to dog parks. That would've been impossible in her younger fighting years. Never straying more than a few feet away, she would lay erect now sporting a grey face that dared any other dog to cross the line.

In time she became frail. Her 'shopping' trips to the local pet stores to buy treats occurred less and less. When she turned fifteen, it became difficult for her to walk. She would collapse on the ground, and where she lay is where I would lay beside her until she recovered. I finally resorted to carrying her sixty-pound frame over my shoulder like a pelt. She lived on a blanket by the fireplace in the den, and often we would take joyrides and trips to the park; never leaving the car, we would watch the passersby like proper senior citizens.

When she started losing her appetite, I would grill her salmon sprinkled with almonds. Her last meals — freshly grilled chicken brought every day from Subway — her favorite.

On December 14, 2014, right after Anthony's 21st birthday party, she 'asked' me to pick her up one last time. I placed her in my lap. I had been petting her for thirty minutes or so when I realized she was no longer breathing. Girl had died looking out the front door, eyes open, still guarding her little piece of real estate, still protecting its occupants, without waivering.

I continued petting her for a while and finally whispered to her, "Well done," and called the family.

My ex-wife showed up in twenty minutes, and together we buried Girl in the backyard with the rest of the bones. My epitaph that day on Facebook reads:

"Girl Dog"
??/??/1998 – 12/14/2014
R.I.P.

Today our family said goodbye to an expensive, people-bitin', trip-stealin', fence-bustin' fleabag, and probably the best friend I'll ever have in my lifetime.

We will miss her every day.

And that was it. I became a dog-less, normal, nine-to-fiver divorcee with grown kids, curious to know what life was like with minimal responsibilities and maximum 'me' time.

That year my boys were twenty-one and twenty-two, fresh out of school and living nearby. They were entering their respective careers, and I had landed a job at a bank that allowed four weeks of paid vacation a year, and for the next two years, I was on it. Alex and I got deep into remote backpacking. I spent my first vacation with him, hiking over forty miles around Shoshone Lake in West Yellowstone. We may have bitten off too much to chew on that father-son trip; I lost my way back to our camp one night after having to move the cooking operation far from the tent to avoid attracting the grizzly bear whose scat we passed earlier in the day, but then promptly lost my way back in the dense dark. The circle of my flashlight illuminated massive wolf tracks, and fear shot through me; I had to press on, the only other option was screaming Alex's name, but that would have likely brought me face to face with that grizzly. A harrowing while later, I saw a beam of light from our tent and breathed a sigh of relief. I arrived back at the tent and found Alex feverishly sick from the swarms of mosquito bites, concurrent with almost being trampled by a full-grown moose after he stumbled out of the tent looking for me while I was over yonder preparing stew.

I spent my next vacation with one of my best friends, Bill, on a motorcycle cruising the Natchez Trace, a scenic state park drive that runs over 400 miles from Natchez, Mississippi to Nashville, Tennessee, a biker's dream road trip. At six foot four, Bill was solid as a tree trunk with a striking mustache; he had about him the look of a barber-shop quartet singer, a talented musician that late in life became a quality control nuclear engineer, exactly the wrong way around. We talked ski trips and cruises.

I had learned to fly at eighteen and had skydived a few times by twenty-three. I had motorcycled in the Alps of Germany.

I had plans that included long stays away from home. I absolutely needed that freedom. I had plans for more big adventures. Big plans. Life was good without a dog.

Until now. Until this Christmas where I stood slightly tipsy and still in shock in my bachelor pad living room looking into two faces. One was Alex's hopeful face; the other belonged to a mongrel who was not about to return me the favor.

CHAPTER 2
BUILDING THE STALAG

HE WAS SKINNY and lanky and if stretched out from nose to tail just shy of six feet long. According to his history, he was one year old, had been adopted only to be returned to a kill shelter where they euthanized close to half their dogs.

They said he was supposed to be a Catahoula. Well, if he is a Catahoula, then I am an Irish Wolfhound. He looked more like a cross between a Saint Bernard and a Black Bear. You've heard of a Chocolate Lab? Zeke looked more like a meth lab and probably had a rap sheet to go with him. Who returns a dog to a kill shelter? I figured if I sent in his DNA, I would get back a scroll as long as he was.

The boys left. It was getting late. Still standing in the living room, I asked Zeke, "What am I gonna do with you?" He answered by casually picking up a butane lighter from the coffee table. Then he glared at me with two brown eyes and slowly crushed it with his powerful jaws; it made a startlingly loud hissing sound.

I wondered if his shots were up to date. I also wondered if we were going to make it through the night.

Without any alternative, I put him in my bedroom to keep him away from any ideas he may have after casing the house. He tromped around in the dark and finally laid down with a *flump* on the floor.

My mind was racing on what tomorrow would be like since my whole life's agenda had been erased. I finally went to sleep after convincing myself I would figure it out tomorrow. Sometime in the night, I woke up to Zeke on the bed with his front paws on my chest staring at me. I slowly pulled the covers over my face wondering if murder had also been left off of his rap sheet and possibly the real reason he was returned to the shelter.

First thing in the morning, I got on the phone to see if the Invisible Fence people were open this late in December. They were, but they could not send anybody out for a week. I reluctantly agreed on a date and time. Alex came by regularly to help. We tried to walk him, which was like flying a kite in a hurricane but not as much fun. We needed a longer leash.

The next night I had planned a holiday dinner party for twenty or so friends. I shut Zeke up in the utility room off the kitchen, and he provided the music for most of the party. When we let him out, I found out in seconds which of my friends were dog people and which were not because it took him about that long to dog sniff every one of them. I could thin out my guest list now and concentrate on the future of this house.

My house is a two-story bungalow built around 1906. The furniture inside is largely antique, with most of the credit going to my mother, who was a collector. Everything is special to me in that it either has a story behind it or it was a gift from someone. I am a minimalist, so there is not much fluff, but the house is full.

Zeke had already brought me a few gifts in his short stay, like the chess pieces I had wagged all the way from Leipzig, Germany, the heads now bit off. As well as chunks of fireplace wood he had chewed that were not actually wood but non-replaceable ceramic logs from the ventless fireplace system and pieces left of the remote control that accompanied the pricey Onkyo sound system that was installed during my last renovation.

I rearranged then removed the 'good' furniture and put all of Mom's glassware in the only safe place I knew on short notice — behind my bed next to the wall in my master bedroom.

Each time Zeke got out of the yard and terrorized the neighborhood, we called it a 'tour,' and each time he was contained, a 'recovery.'

Zeke had two 'tours' and two 'recoveries' his first week before the Invisible Fence people showed up.

We kept two permanent posts up with his mug shot on the humane shelter's Facebook site:

ZEKE wants everyone to know ... He got a Home for The Holidays!! #Adopted

If anybody has seen this dog, please DM us as he was last seen in the Sylvan Park neighborhood area. Thank you.

When the Invisible Fence folks finally arrived, they estimated the job to be around 1,400 dollars. It would involve running an underground cable around my front and backyard and include two weeks of training with the dog. I got out my credit card, and they started that day. Zeke was the gift that kept on giving. This four-legged behemoth was a round-the-clock, full-time job that had to be taken in shifts. The boys helped out, and that allowed me to do things like run errands, but they were not always able to be there. On one of those days, I had to leave Zeke home alone to make a grocery run. I quickly made two trips from the car with bags and later estimated that those trips took under one minute total. While putting the groceries up, I counted only one loaf of bread when I was sure I bought two. I went back to the car and found nothing but then remembered walking by something lying under Zeke, who was half sleeping on the couch. I went back in to check and pulled an empty bread wrapper out from under him. How can a whole loaf of bread be eaten in thirty seconds? That is when I realized how much this dog loved bread. I was learning things about Zeke in those first few days. He was not mean-spirited but rather aloof and distanced. We did not bond at all, none of us. He seemed to be biding his time freeloading, camped out on the couch until he got his next gig. He tolerated us and kept his own set of rules. Once I tried to get him out of a 'nice' chair in the living room and attempted to lay down the law, threatening him with shouts and hand gestures. He just looked at me with a disdained curiosity. When I got close, he growled and casually showed me his incisors. He seemed comfortable and mildly entertained by my dance of frustration. I had cornered a tree stump with teeth. Finally, I just gave up and took a picture of him with my phone. That picture would later be used as a cautionary tale and as reference for a large oil painting that still hangs prominently in my house and is called, 'Zeke's Chair.'

When the bonus trainer arrived from the Invisible Fence deal, she turned out to be a slight German girl who knew a lot about dogs and fences. She started by giving me a lesson on the fact that it was more about training me because the dog would figure it out himself. She walked me around the newly laid underground fence and explained how the dog would immediately stop when he felt the electricity and back away. We then went inside.

She made some adjustments on the special collar and smiled, "Und now vee vill zee how dee dog doz, ok?"

I opened the back door, Zeke looked out, glanced back at us, then back to the door, then finally got up and slowly trotted outside. We gave him a few minutes then went to check on his progress. We found him lying directly on top of the live wire fence line, casually chewing on a stick. She looked concerned. I got worried.

She said, "Open zee gate!"

I opened it. He looked disinterested.

She was flabbergasted, "Dat ist not zee reaction dat I vaz looking for! Stay here viz zee dog und I vill return in un moment, pleez."

I stayed outside and caught a glimpse of Zeke, who was now walking out the gate. "Zeke ... ZEEEEEK!" I tried to catch him, and he took off in a trot. I ran inside the house, grabbed the leash, and raced out the front door yelling his name. I could hear the girl behind me shouting words in German, but I couldn't make them out. I searched until I heard a big dog scuffle a few doors down. It sounded bad. *Oh God, please don't let him kill anybody!* To my relief, I found Zeke sparring with two other dogs through the neighbor's fence and not the bloodbath I had feared. I took the leash and lassoed him like a calf. *Jesus Christ!!*

I was gassed. After a few minutes, the trainer caught up with us, and together we coerced him back to the house. Back inside, we took his collar off, and she opened the back of it and turned up the dials to the highest setting. "Eef zis setting don't verk you get refund, ok?" *Lady, if this setting don't work, they can study him in a zoo!* She put the collar back on and made sure that the electrodes had good contact with his neck.

Free again, Zeke traveled outside with his new collar toward the exit, once again toward the neighbor's yard. I found him a few minutes later rolled over on the fence line, stunned. He was done. The collar worked. The neighborhood was safe.

She said she would check back in a week and to call her if I had questions and drove off. Zeke and I went back outside in the backyard. Emotions came to me out of nowhere, and I sat down. Zeke looked at me, snorted, and walked off. Now he could have the freedom of the whole yard instead of a few rooms guarded by people working shifts. Tears welled up as I sat there on the grass, watching him inspect his newfound digs. He barely noticed me.

"YOU'RE WELCOME!" I shouted.

"YOU COULD WIN A MILLION DOLLARS IN VEGAS OVER A DECK OF CARDS WITH THAT FACE!!"

He looked unimpressed. This dog was growing on me.

CHAPTER 3

MIXED FEELINGS

ZEKE'S UNIQUE CHARACTER made us all wonder what kind of life he had before us. He trusted no one but wasn't afraid of anything. We found out on New Year's Eve that he loved fireworks. Although he could jump ten feet and run like a deer, he was usually calm and careful with his size. He paid little attention to people or other dogs. Squirrels were his obsession and cats. He could not tolerate a cat even a block away.

His main entertainment was gobbling up lighters, but that was just an hors d'oeuvre. The first time I saw him throw up, it was like I had emptied a vacuum cleaner bag of cigar butts, cellophane wrappers, and plastic pieces of various colors and sizes. I began buying reading glasses in bags instead of one at a time, as they were a delicacy of his.

He was confident in his environment and gentle unless provoked. You could pull on him but never push him. He gained another ten pounds that winter.

I tried many walking devices: chokers, spikers, chainers, but he never liked the neck thing. I tried the gentle leader on his snout and almost lost a hand. Put on a harness and almost said goodbye to my knees.

I finally arrived at the technique of a regular large collar with the leash wrapped under the belly and looped over his back, so it kind of pulled him sideways, which he tolerated.

When it got warmer in the spring, I took him on the local greenway. It was located a half- mile from the house, and it was about a three-mile loop. We walked the whole thing almost every day. We could walk it three times a day, yet he never cared to rest. I was about the only one that could contain him on a walk. He gained another twenty-five pounds over the summer.

One day, Anthony called me at work saying he had tried to walk him when Zeke spotted the big yellow stray cat that lived in the neighborhood. That had resulted in a major, major tour. I immediately got in the car and sped home to start the search. After about an hour, I received a phone call from someone who had read my phone number on his collar. Apparently, he had been doing laps around the greenway the whole time. He had run away to the only place nearby he knew. I parked close to the greenway and waited. Sure enough, I saw the tip of his tail. He saw me and jumped in the car.

Throughout the first few months, he tolerated us and his new environment. If I left him for long periods, I would come back and get no response. *I missed you so much I'm gonna wag my tail until it flies off!* says every other normal dog I have owned, but not Zeke.

He came into my room one night and jumped on the bed. It was the first time he had ever volunteered to do this without the cover of darkness.

I whispered to him, "What did they do to you in that shelter, buddy?"

He responded with a deep exhale and was out like a light. I drifted off to sleep, imagining him fighting for food, being pushed into tight cages, and being left alone for days.

Not long after he had settled in, in the middle of the night, he woke me up dog dreaming, running, jerking, and making "Brfff ... Brfff Brfff ..." sounds while moving the entire bed with his thrashing.

I smiled, wondering where he was off to in dreamland. Legs kicking and jerking, he was going off somewhere ... then off the bed he went, CRRRRRAAASH!!!

The sound was like somebody had dropped a glass china cabinet on the hardwood floor ... that's when I realized that was exactly where I had stored my mother's delicate glass china.

I jumped out of bed and turned on the light. There he was, blinking his eyes looking confused, sprawled out in a large pile of scattered glassware. The last precious glassware that existed of my dear mother's estate.

I angrily stumbled to the bathroom, flashed on the lights, and looked at myself in the mirror, "YOU are getting rid of him in the morning. Did you hear me dog, you are outta here!"

When I came back into the room, I had changed to a different creature. Whatever I said or did must have reached Zeke's brain; he was listening now. Maybe this is the way I should look all the time — like a wild deranged killer. Maybe he will listen now; maybe he will sit; maybe he will even shake my hand.

"GET THE HELL OUTTA MY ROOM, ZEKE. NOW!!!"

He did not know what he had done, but he knew it had set off enough of my buttons, and he did not want to test them anymore. Zeke lowered his tail and left in a hurry

Aaawwgggghh. I did NOT want a dog! Especially this one!

In the morning, I discovered a miracle of miracles. After examining every piece of the estate glassware, not a single piece was broken. It was like Mom had come in during the night and fixed it. That is what I like to believe anyway.

But I had to do something with Zeke.

I did not return him to the shelter. Not yet anyway, I just was not yet willing to let down my son, so instead I started taking him to dog parks. Reluctant at first with dogs, he was awkward. When he saw two dogs roughhousing, he thought they were fighting and tried to break them up. The dog park people started calling him the "Sheriff." He would play with only a few dogs he got to know well. There was Tug, Hailey, Wally, Jude, and a big Great Dane named Harley. He learned to drag Harley down by grabbing his collar with his teeth and pulling him over. It must have seemed reasonable to him to even the playing field by shorting Harley's stature; not normal dog behavior, but we continued going with a prayer.

Mainly, Zeke liked the squirrels in the park. He would quickly get bored with the dogs and study the tree limbs for movement. When he spotted a squirrel, he would let out a yell like he had been hit by a car and try heroically to climb the tree. Once, he spotted one on a fence rail about as high as my head and jumped clear over the fence rails to get it. Everybody just stopped what they were doing. I do not think any one of them had ever seen a dog jump that high over a fence to get *out* of the dog park.

After three months of daily dog parking it, we settled into a kind of detente. I was getting used to him, and he to me. Until one night, after a big day of romping, Zeke stole a loaf of bread off the kitchen counter and dragged it to the sofa in the living room. I followed him into the room to get it away, and he threw me a long low growl. I scolded him, and he snarled. This was becoming a futile showdown.

My son, hearing all the snarling and scolding, came into the room and told *me* to leave it, but I was tired of being ruled by a dog.

I slapped the couch and told Zeke to, "Drop it! No, bad dog!"

All the other tips and tricks that people have advised me to do flashed through my brain, but all I could think of was to yell, "ZEKE, I SAID DROP IT!!"

When he continued to ignore me, I took decisive action and made a grab for the loaf.

As my hand came close to the bread, he snapped and bit down hard and fast. I felt his teeth but did not register the damage. He gave me a warning growl and showed me his teeth, his bloody teeth. And that is when I looked down at what he had done to my hand. There was a two-inch slash about a half-inch deep, starting just below my index finger down to the base of my thumb. Blood was now gushing down my arm.

Still holding the loaf of bread in his paws, Zeke seemed to grin, daring me again. But I was done. Cooked, like him and the electric fence, I was done. Never had I given up on any dog, but this was it.

I went to the bathroom to dress my wound. Thankfully, he didn't snap any of the tendons, but it was bleeding too much for any bandage I had, so I ran some hydrogen peroxide over it and wrapped it tourniquet-style as tight as I could until I could get to a doctor.

I walked back to the living room, where Zeke had finished his bread. Anthony and I were able to get him out the back door. I turned the outside light off and left him there.

The next day I received ten stitches and was contacted by Animal Control. When I came home, Zeke was lying in the same place on the back porch where we left him the night before; he had barely moved. That day he did not let out a single bark, and nobody said a word to him. He had earned some serious timeout. After dinner, I left the light off again. Anthony slid him food and water and came back into the house. Same thing the next day. No light, no communication. Just one food and water visit.

Over the next few days, I thought about it and decided to give him up for adoption. He was just too dangerous, and at the speed he was growing he was going to get me sued or take a limb. Nobody would be against my decision. The family would understand. The shelter would understand. The neighborhood would understand. And I *know* dog park Harley would understand.

I had tried my damnedest to accept my Christmas 'gift' but failed miserably. I wondered if Zeke would understand.

I went to the kitchen and looked out the door. It was a warm day with a bright blue sky. Zeke had not barked, moved, or hardly eaten since we had left him in that spot three days ago. He just lay there, a shell of a dog, unmoving, like a sad ornamental cement lawn dog.

I rapped on the glass, and his eyes slowly turned up to look at me. I went to the pantry and got two pieces of bread. I opened the door and sat on the steps. I showed him the bread, which he initially ignored. I motioned for him to come to the steps. He got up and lumbered toward me before sitting down right in front of my feet, his eyes down.

Before giving him the bread, I showed him my newly stitched hand; he sniffed it.

Then I spoke, "This is not what friends do to each other, buddy."

He gently took the bread from my hand and ate it. I offered him some water, and he drank it.

Then I put him in the car and took him to the biggest dog park in the county. Still not saying a word, we parked and made our way to the entrance. I opened the gate, led him in, and took off his leash.

It was over fifteen acres with a hidden fence. Zeke looked up at me; as far as he knew, I was letting him go. Giving him his ultimate freedom. Saying goodbye.

I started walking away to see what he would do. I turned around and saw he was following me at a distance. I stopped and waited till he caught up to me, and I noticed for the first time he was staring directly into my eyes. I believe he was trying to read my mind.

I started walking in another direction, and he followed me again. He moved closer, then closer. Pretty soon, he was matching me step for step.

CHAPTER 4

A COMPROMISE OF TRUST

NOTHING HAD PREPARED me for Zeke. No books, no trainers, or well-meaning advice from friends had pierced his stony resolve. I had to show him in my own way that there were rules that existed and needed to be followed for the sake of harmony. We just had to discover them together. As he started considering the house his home instead of his prison, he regarded it as such. He had his furniture, and I had mine. If he found food, it was his and vice versa. If I was dumb enough to leave a loaf of bread within his reach, then I quietly watched him engulf it. I could sit next to him on the couch, eat a whole pizza, and he would not look at me. I did not own a dog; we just shared a house together tentatively like college roommates from different countries. Wondering if he could be trained with a bribe, I got some bread, and after several minutes I taught him to 'Sit.' He didn't like doing it, but he begrudgingly obeyed to get a piece of bread. It was the only command he knew. Maybe that was the start of getting him to trust my words.

Eventually, I arranged the furniture to be more dog-friendly. I bought him the largest dog bed I could find and made sure the color matched *his* chair. In his bed, he kept his toys, firewood, and lighters. He really seemed to like his yard. And he loved to ride in the car with all the windows open; it only took him two lessons to learn that jumping out while moving was a lot less fun than it looked.

Having the house to myself and free, unfettered bachelorhood was slowly evaporating into the past. We were cautiously settling into a new normal.

Until one Sunday afternoon, I was laid out on the couch about to watch the first NFL game of the season when the TV went blank. I turned the cable off and on and was letting it do a self-check when I heard Anthony yell from upstairs, "Dad, what happened to the Internet?"

Hmmm. No cable, no Internet either at the same time? I called Comcast, who did a system check over the phone that lasted several minutes. No luck. They scheduled a service guy to come to the house in about an hour.

That gave me some time to clean up the place. The weather was great, and I had kept Zeke outside since morning, which was something I rarely did. We had not walked, been to the dog park, or shared much all day. He seemed to be quietly happy with whatever he was doing out there, and that made me feel good.

Me, I had been a slob leaving plates and clothes lying about. Ah, the joys of an all-male household.

I had just put everything away when a white van pulled into the driveway. The service guy smiled, and I directed him to the box at the side of the house. He came back in less than two minutes, saying he had located the problem.

"Wow, that was fast. What do think it is?" I asked.

He answered, "Sir, I opened up the box and noticed that you don't have any cable that's connected to the house."

I scoffed, "Sure, I do. I was watching football less than an hour ago."

Nervous, he said, “Sir, well, I mean, well, you don’t have any now. All the cables look like they have been eaten off. Chewed up.”

Uh oh. I could feel the top of my head heating up.

Panicked, I asked, “Did you leave the box open?”

Before he could answer, I was running out the door to the side of the house.

There he was. He had a mouth full of cables. It looked like Zeke had been playing with spaghetti. I dashed back inside the kitchen and found the bread. When I came out again, the guy was gently reaching for the cables in Zeke’s open mouth.

I yelled, “NO!! DON’T DO THAT! STOP WHERE YOU ARE! Now back away slowly.”

The guy froze. Then slowly took a few steps back, never taking his eyes off of Zeke. Then he stood frozen like a statue in the same bent-over position.

“ZEEK ... SIT!” He obeyed. I pitched my piece of bread out a few yards and watched as Zeke slowly let the cables fall from his mouth, then lumbered over and gulped the bread.

The guy quickly gathered up his cables, grabbed his tools, and made for the fence.

Too loudly. I replied, “If it’s all the same to you, I think I’ll change to a dish.”

As soon as the van pulled away, I got on the phone, canceled my cable service, and ordered satellite. The rule I learned that day was simple. No dog park for Zeke? Then no football for me. I decided that we needed some joint hobbies if we were going to keep this relationship healthy.

Zeke had gained another twenty pounds; we were both needing some adventure in our lives. The greenway was getting repetitive. The dog park was mostly full of people that talked or typed on their phones while their dogs ran around and entertained themselves. Zeke got bored quickly of the same patch of dirt, and I bored quickly of watching people watch their smartphones. We both enjoyed walking, but we needed new landscapes to explore. I thought about how I had bonded with Alex while we went backpacking on long excursions. Do not get me wrong. I like people and have many friends, but I equally enjoy being by myself, for days at a time. The best way that I know to do that is to get lost in the woods.

So, the next day I corralled him to the car, rolled all the windows down, and drove to the largest park in the city. It was hundreds of acres with many trails to follow. I put Zeke on a twenty-six-foot retractable leash and let him lead. I noticed a different quickness in his step. He was in his element. His world had opened up; I could sense his excitement level rising dramatically. When we passed other dogs and people, Zeke did not give them notice. He seemed intent with purpose; perhaps he was brought up in the sticks somewhere that looked like this. He went up and down dry riverbeds on a mission; his head was on a swivel. When he pulled me up steep banks, I was just a load, nothing else.

"Hold on, buddy, this ain't a race." But it was for him. I realized I was in the wrong park. We needed to go find a much bigger one.

I waited until the next nice weekend, and this time we headed off to Savage Gulf State Park an hour and a half away.

Zeke hung his head out of the window most of the way, ears flapping, his nose to the wind, tail wagging with something like a smile.

When we got to the South Rim trailhead, he put his nose straight up, sniffed the air, and paced back and forth in the back seat.

When I let him out, he was barely containable as we hit the trail. I carried food and water in a daypack, and we were off.

I did not have a map or a compass and really did not know where we were going. We just were. He was practically in a gallop with me holding on to the leash twenty-six feet behind him, trying my best to keep up.

Zeke turned right, followed a blue-blazed sidetrack, and after about 100 yards of diving through blind curves, skidded to an abrupt stop. The leash went slack, allowing me to catch my breath. He stood frozen on a piece of rock atop a high bluff that looked out over a beautiful sunlit valley below. Another step would have sent him 200-feet to the bottom.

"That was a blue marker back there, buddy, and you're color blind. I need to take the lead this time."

He looked back at me, whined once, and started back at the same pace as before but a little more cautious than before.

When we got to the original fork, he slowed and looked confused.

I passed him on the right and said, "This way!"

Then took off again on the white blaze. He followed me briefly then squeezed by to take the lead. Shortly we came upon another blue-blazed fork, he stopped and looked at me. I ran by him shouting, "This way!" We continued down the correct trail at full speed.

After about two hours of these antics, I found a sidetrack that led to another bluff where we stopped and ate some lunch. A sandwich for me, some holistic dog kibble I had been suckered into buying for him. Atop our perch, he was fascinated by the view. After lunch, we just sat there on the rock ledge high above the trees, listening to the sounds.

I said softly, "So, we got stuff in common, huh?"

He looked right into my eyes, tilting his head to a forty-five, his lip hitched up on a tooth giving him an odd, goofy grin.

I looked straight ahead at the distant North Rim bluffs a mile away on the other side of the gorge, and Zeke followed my gaze. The soft roar of the wind rushed through the trees in the valley and cooled our faces as we watched a hawk coast on the breeze below. It was flying beneath us. He was calm, alert, and seemingly in heaven.

I smiled, "Well, buddy, I guess we do."

We continued at a slower, more deliberate pace along the ridge. He let me lead this time, especially when encountering forks in the trail that involved markers. I let him lead when anything involved sounds or smells. He once stopped so abruptly I almost ran into him. I looked around carefully through the thickness and there saw the faint outline of a deer about twenty feet to our right. I would never have caught sight of it had he not pointed. He put his nose high in the air and sniffed, then tensed his haunches and stood poised like a runner waiting for the starter's pistol.

I quickly looped my end of the leash around a small tree beside me seconds before the deer bounded up the ridge. Zeke bolted and the leash snapped taught. I had barely gotten my hands free of the leash before the tree started to bow.

Zeke bellowed his delight and again tested the tree. Now he realized the woods were full of four-legged creatures like him. This was the first time I had seen this dog truly comfortable with his surroundings. This was where he was connecting on a level that only he understood. I was in his world now. I would carry the food and the water while he led me up steep beauty. I was the load he was learning to trust at the forks.

The trails led us through mountain laurel mazes of leafy brush, then would open into wide, grassy, flat areas where we would stop for water or to rest. He never wanted to rest for long and would look at me for direction, then tug me up another hill.

We found a swiftly moving river with a rocky shore that led to a waterfall. I noticed that Zeke avoided the water. Had he never swum? Apparently, his instinct told him to stay away. Or maybe someone had tried drowning him? He would drink it but not dare step in.

I lost both the track of time and my bearings. It had been stupid to come this far without a map. The sun had dropped lower in the sky, and the route I chose to get us back had been wrong. But I wound up spotting at the coolest little campsite nestled in the deep shade right in front of me. On a short post, there was a sign that read, 'Sawmill.' I took a picture of it with my phone and turned around to find our way back.

If you are an avid hiker, keep your senses and stay on the trail; you can usually find your way back with the help of the sun's location, and a little praying does not hurt. I attribute our success in navigating our way back to the latter. When we finally limped to the parking lot, ours was the only vehicle in sight. I opened the back door, Zeke crawled in, and in no time was passed out, drooling heavily on the seat.

We slept that night together on my bed in the master bedroom. This time he did not move. Sometime in the night, I woke up to find him next to my side. All six feet of him breathing slow and steady in a soft snore. That was the last thing I remembered until the sun came up the next morning.

The next day we went back to the dog park. Zeke lumbered around the dogs for a while, but there were none he recognized. Suddenly, out of nowhere came a large pit bull that charged him and bit him on the backside. I came running up at the same time the pit's owner grabbed his dog and roughly smacked it on the head; he hooked a leash on its collar and dragged it away.

I looked over Zeke and saw no broken skin. He was agitated but had not reciprocated. I was glad. I had already been to the doctor twice more since the bread incident with stitched hands from breaking up dog skirmishes. The last time I was there, the doctor gave me the rest of the suture kit and told me to practice on raw chicken skin and learn to do it myself.

Zeke wandered off to find squirrels. Ten minutes later, from the corner of my eye, I caught a blur heading straight for Zeke. I quickly yelled at the top of my lungs, "ZEEK, SIT!" Zeke slowly complied with his back turned toward the onrushing dog. He was learning to trust my words. But I had misjudged the situation badly.

The blood-starved pit hit Zeke in the backside of his head like a hammer and clamped down on his neck for the fun of killing, devouring his flesh like a vicious lion. Zeke never had a chance.

CHAPTER 5

PICASSO'S PALETTE

MY FIRST FLIGHT instructor was a crusty old gent that lived and worked out of a brick terminal on a small grass airstrip. His name was Roald Boen. He was from Nebraska and had a thick northern accent and flowing white hair. I would hang around the airport, and he would pay me for small jobs. I would clean and sweep out the small hangers that housed the tiny single-engine planes that were the tools of his trade. I would spend my last dollar on flight lessons and then watch him for hours as he tinkered with plane engines. I would sit and listen as he told me stories about the close calls he had in the war and tales of crop dusting so low he had to avoid plowed furrows in the fields. He had been a fighter pilot and had trained pilots in World War II. I was seventeen and hung on his every word.

He drove a rusty heap of a van, and I never saw him wearing anything but dirty coveralls, but he was one of the most generous men I would come to know that would shape my life forever. He would teach me to fly, and he would teach me about fear.

One day we were sitting inside the terminal, a thick layer of stratus hung barely a few hundred feet above our heads. It was a grey, wet day with thunder booming off in the distance. We were listening to the crackling Unicom radio, not saying much; I was in a depressed funk after the loss of a girlfriend whose name I cannot remember now.

He winked at me and said, “Let’s go; I want to show you something.”

We walked over the grassy field with barely a word between us. While we pushed his old red Cessna 150 out of the hanger, the wheel pants caught him on the back of his foot.

“Ouch!” he shouted, “Damn it! I hate airplanes!”

This comment threw me a little off guard. His whole life and career had been formed around airplanes. He had flown fighters, crop dusters, and scrappy kids like me around for decades. I asked him to explain. We got in and strapped on our belts.

He said, “Airplanes are expensive, loud, dirty, clumsy, and when they break down, whew, they’re hell to fix.”

Then he opened the window and shouted, “CLEAR!”, clicked the Master on, and pulled the starter.

The propeller jerked a few times while the engine spat and finally fired into a roaring idle. Standing on one brake, he throttled it around and headed past the windsock on the other end of the muddy strip. Whipping it around one final time, he pushed the throttle to the dashboard. We bounced a few times on the muddy grass until we could feel nothing but air below us as we slowly climbed up into the soup.

“Yep, nothin’ dirtier than fixin’ a damn airplane.” He was calmly griping about dirt, and I was glued to the seat, looking through a wet windshield at zero visibility, scared to death. He spoke again, “Picasso probably hated his messy paint palette too. You ever tried to clean an oil paint palette? Yuck!” He then he explained the analogy. “I don’t like airplanes or the messy palettes, but I sure do like what you can do with ’em.”

The plane buffeted through the dark nothingness as he went about this and that. And then the darkness around us started to get lighter, then lighter still. When we broke through the tops of the clouds, the little plane stopped its buffeting and leveled off in the smooth, clean air.

The bright, billowy stratus below us beckoned and stretched to the horizons in all directions. It was as if we could land on its soft surface and play on its hills. The sky ahead of us was a light, perfect blue, and above us, a more perfect darker shade of blue. Twenty minutes before, we had been under a drizzling dark and dreary cloud. It was this same cloud layer that was now providing us with so much wonder and delight.

I relaxed my grip on the seat and glanced over at Roald, who, with his everlasting smile fixed on his face, leaned over and said, "Look over there now."

He was concentrating on the plane's angle to the sun. Gentle on the controls, he tipped the wings to angle with the clouds but kept the same heading.

I looked out my window and thought I was seeing things. On the cloud to my right lay a cross. It was moving at our same speed on the surface of the cloud and followed us along over every billowy bump. Around the cross there was a beautiful rainbow. A whole rainbow that surrounded it in a complete circle. It was the shadow of our plane perfectly angled with the sun.

"That's what I wanted you to see." He said, "That's the Pilot's Cross. God's way of letting you know there is nothing to fear, you're never alone."

CHAPTER 6
INTO THE WILD

THE SIGHT OF two massive animals fighting with the intent to kill is a primal astonishment to the senses. Initially it is a fast flurry of who can get to the neck or side first. The tender underbelly must be protected at all costs. There is nothing a slower human can do except watch it unfold for the first minute or two. You can shout all you want but the snarls get louder.

The shouting had captured the attention of all the fifty or so dog owners at the park who came rushing to see the horrible fracas. They scrambled to find and protect their own dogs first, then to try to help.

I had earlier given Zeke the command to "sit," to "stay," and for the first time he had trusted and obeyed my words. Now he was dealing with the consequences of ignoring his own instincts and listening to me.

The pit ripped into Zeke's side. Zeke whipped around and grabbed his aggressor's ear and began pulling it off. The pit then tore into the top of Zeke's forearm and latched. Somehow Zeke twisted and now had half the pit's head in his mouth and began to tear away the loose skin on the side of its jaw.

The pit's face began to disappear in an ugly, impossibly contorted headlock exposing long stretches of the insides of skin. The pit's eyes were closed as the fight stalled for a moment. Four of us then attempted to pull Zeke away from the pit, but Zeke was slowly squeezing the life out of the brute he held by the head. The pit threw his back legs up trying to regain his footing, but it was no use. The pit's owner started kicking Zeke in the ribs with his big leather boots. Zeke just watched him from the side of his eye while clamping down on his dog. I knew that look on Zeke's face. It was like he was thinking, "*You're next. But first, your dog.*"

People were shouting and screaming; dust was flying as someone grabbed the pit's owner by the shoulders drawing him back away from the fight so we could pull Zeke off the pit.

We finally succeeded in getting them apart and leashed. I led Zeke several feet away and just embraced him to keep him protected. There were some shouts at the pit's owner, who quickly left with his dog. I am not sure how the pit fared, but Zeke was a bloody mess, and so was I.

Someone came and brought us a whole box of wipes that we used to try to clean the blood off. There were not enough.

Even in his state, Zeke looked up at the trees for another squirrel. He was cut everywhere. The gash on his forearm was deep, blood oozing out so fast I knew I had to find a hospital quickly or he would bleed to death.

I carried Zeke out of the dog park, wrapped him in my jacket, and placed him in the back of my car. I raced to the emergency entrance of the Veterinarian hospital where he was admitted and put on the table. I was not allowed inside. They had him anesthetized and immediately into surgery.

I paced the waiting area for two hours and finally received word that he was alive and asleep. They said he had been a lightweight to the drugs, so they were keeping him overnight.

The next morning, I got a call from the vet saying he was going to live but had several stitches, the worst being the deep gash in his forearm. When I picked him up, they led him out the door, and he spotted me right away in the full waiting room. He sported an Elizabethan-sized cone bigger than any lampshade I had in the house. I have to admit; after that epic fight for life, I admired his matter-of-fact trot out the door, his 'let's just get on with it' attitude.

At home, the cone proved to be a nightmare. He was so wide I had to rearrange the furniture, but that still did not prevent him from scooting a leather chair into the French doors, knocking out a pane of glass in the dining room.

He could not get to his stitches, but they were coming out anyway, and he was bleeding so much I had to call my local vet and make an appointment to put them back in. My vet did a much better job with the stitching. I watched him as he put a knee against Zeke's chest and pulled so hard at the sutures you could hear them groan and squeak together inside the skin. I held Zeke's head as he watched. And yet, he uttered not one yelp. In fact, I have never seen Zeke whimper or complain while in pain. I accidentally stepped on his tail once with all my weight, and he just stared up at me silently with a quizzical expression like, "Did you mean to step on my tail?"

The vet told us to hold off on hiking for a few weeks while Zeke healed. I would soon learn; he could fix his wounds but not his spirit. Zeke was becoming even more silent and withdrawn as if all the dog in him had retreated.

But by the end of three weeks, Zeke still ignored all the pampering and quietly became a complacent house dog. He learned to be ultra-careful with his headgear, and I was suckered into buying more holistic food. The best this time. But still, he seemed miserable. Barely eating. Zeke was depressed, simple as that. When his ribs started showing, I knew I needed a plan. I could not just sit there watching him fail. I was the one, after all, that had directed him to sit, to stay.

That night, I downloaded the AllTrails app for my phone and started studying dog-friendly trails that were available in the state. I joined the group 'Hiking with Dogs' on Facebook.

I learned there were many dog people worldwide who shared the passion of losing themselves with their trusty companions in the backwoods.

There were incredible pictures of every terrain imaginable, with a human always accompanied by a dog smiling and sometimes donning its own backpack. I decided we had to get back out there. Where he had seemed more connected, more dog.

But first, we had to train for it and get Zeke ready. After the vet removed the stitches and gave us the green light, we hit the greenway.

The bikers and joggers were there, and of course, it was crowded. Flashy shorts, road rage, and dogs on short leashes were not our cup of tea. But we could ignore all that. This was just for exercise, boosting his stamina, practice for the real thing. We were both out of shape and needed to get our legs back.

I remembered back to the small campground we had passed, and that is where we were eventually headed. But first, we had to get stronger and then get some supplies.

When we got up to ten miles a day, I started planning the trip. I downloaded a trail map of the South Rim, obtained a backcountry permit for Sawmill from the Ranger's Station, and headed to REI for supplies.

Early morning that next Saturday, we headed back to Savage Gulf — this time with a frame backpack, tent, water filter, and a mission. When we pulled into the parking lot at the trailhead, there were no cars. *Perfect!*

At the tiny station, I showed the park ranger my permit, got him to snap our picture with my phone, and we headed off. The trek was going to be long, and this was no greenway romp; I had about thirty pounds on my back. Zeke was almost fully recovered physically, and I did not want to push him more than either of us was ready. We could not afford to get lost.

Zeke started with his usual gallop but found that the load I carried resulted in his end of the leash being heavier this time. With the supplies on my back slowing him down, he was much easier to manage. The first fork he remembered to go left but needed help with the next two.

About three miles later, he stopped and sniffed on the ground in a wide circle. After watching him do this for a minute, I realized this was precisely where he had jumped the deer over a month ago.

We ate lunch on a familiar bluff. Zeke enjoyed the sights and got bolder with his footing on the ledge. When we came to the waterfall, Zeke held back. I tied him to a tree and went to filter some water. I filled three liters which added to our weight, but we did not have much farther to go.

With our trail map, it was easy to find the small campground, and it was not long before I was standing in front of the short sign again that said, 'Sawmill.' We were totally alone in the woods, and it was late afternoon.

The permit we had assured us that we would not have any other visitors anywhere near us that night. I felt safe, plus I had a pretty stout security dog if I heard any banjos.

Zeke got antsy when the sun started going down. I directed him to lay down, and he soon became mesmerized by the campfire. I kept an eye on him as he watched me pitch the tent. Our tent was a two-man, and it fit us to a tee. Zeke tipped the scale around 100 pounds, and I weigh about 190 pounds on any given day, so it was a perfect fit. I set up the tiny pocket stove to boil water to get my supper going.

The katydids were first, then the crickets, and finally, the frogs provided a soothing musical backdrop as dusk came on. A small lantern hung from a tree, illuminating Zeke and the tent just behind him. He finally relaxed; his feet crossed in front of him.

Starved, I finished my freeze-dried chow mane and poured him some food and water in two foldable bowls. He eagerly ate and drank everything in front of him. Pleased to see him eat again with gusto, we both settled in front of the roaring fire to ponder the evening. I thought about our car parked thirty miles from the nearest service station and the fact that we were miles from the car, deep in the hills of East Tennessee, with nothing holding us together but twenty-six feet of leash. I wondered if I took the leash off if he would still stay close to me or run for his life. Listening to the crickets and frogs and his soft snore, I concluded that there was a good possibility that he might stay by my side. Until the first deer he sighted, then he would be halfway to Kentucky.

I drank the half-pint of bourbon I had brought in a flask and toasted the night. One cigar later and a zip of the tent, we were both stretched out, me in my sleeping bag and him at my side; Zeke was asleep within two minutes. Throughout the whole ordeal of this day, Zeke never uttered one sound.

Early the next morning, it started a gentle rain. I quickly unzipped the flap, pulled my shoes inside checking for spiders, millipedes, or any other hermits, then donned them and went outside to begin the day.

I carefully poured some water into a pan, balanced it on the pocket stove, and brought it to a boil. Zeke patiently watched as I poured the boiling water over my instant egg breakfast in a bag. He did not beg, just curious. He tended to eat a big meal once a day, and that was sufficient. I never fed him any of my food, so he never had any expectation of it and his manners were good. If he found food on his own, that was most definitely his. We had an unspoken treaty.

Once the rain had stopped, I squeezed everything back into my backpack and poured out most of the excess water we had to reduce weight. Zeke, hitched to the same tree he had been the night before, was taking it all in. He never took his eyes off me. I do not know if it was a friendly stare; I think it was more of a "What are you doing and is this keeping me hitched to a tree thing necessary?" kind of stare. Before long, we were back on the trail headed back to the car.

When we got to a waterfall, I turned to him, curious if the roar of the water was spooking him. He ignored it at first, but when we angled toward it, he tensed up, became more alert. I hitched him to a tree on the edge of the falls, unbuckled and slid off the backpack, and sat it on the ground. I stripped down to my undies, took one more look at him as if to steady us both, and dove into the water.

When I came up for air, he was going ballistic. His "ARK AARF ARK" was constant as he tested all the limits of the tree. I hoped his leash would hold but pressed on with a long breaststroke.

I swam up and down in front of him and then got out on the bank and stretched. God, that water was cold. I calmly got dressed, filtered a little water to last us the rest of the way, and donned the backpack. When I untied Zeke, he sniffed me and then quickly turned up the trail leading me away from the water. I hoped he would remember that I did not disappear, drown, or abandon him that day.

CHAPTER 7

WET FEET

THE LOCAL GREENWAY bordered a small creek at one side where Zeke had never been; refusing to go anywhere near bodies of water, he avoided it like the plague.

After a year of hikes, backyard escapes, and pilfered turkey carcasses, I felt Zeke was ready to conquer his fear of water.

I Googled 'Life jackets for dogs' and found them at my local PetSmart, so I put Zeke in the car, and off we went.

He opened the automatic doors to the store himself and walked in on his leash. The salesperson showed us the life jackets, helped us with his size ("just give me the biggest you got"), and took it up front for purchase.

There was one thing I had not factored in on that trip to the store. While walking to the front where the check-out registers were located, Zeke noticed the birds, and that is all it took to get his feet slipping sideways on the floor. Even holding him with a death grip, on the slick floor, he still made it to one of the cages. The birds began to flutter and bang on the glass, and that absolutely set him off.

I managed to yank him to the next aisle where he spotted the cats, and all hell broke loose; I quickly changed direction as Zeke, unable to gain traction, galloped in place in the floor like a cartoon dog. Three clerks ran over to help.

I somehow wrenched a credit card out of my wallet and threw it and the life jacket to one of them, yelling, "WE'LL TAKE IT!!" as I pulled Zeke to the door in a half slide, half drag. They rang up the purchase, threw the card and jacket to me without a bag which I caught with my free hand, then wrestled Zeke through the door with all my might.

I shouted back through clenched teeth, "THANKS, SORRY ABOUT THE BIRDS!"

At least we now had a life jacket, although Zeke had probably rather we'd bought one or two birds and a cat.

On the next trip to the greenway, Zeke sported his new jacket. On our first lap around, we did not go near the water. By the second lap, he was getting thirsty, so I decided it was time we went to the creek. Zeke was seriously afraid of water; the time had come, and I felt he was ready and slowly approached the water.

He cautiously went toward the edge and lapped up some water. I waded in and started splashing. He barked and carried on in an attempt to get me to change my mind, but I just ignored him and encouraged him to come in for some fun. He paced back and forth like an angry lion and then stopped, looked at me, at the water, and then he ventured to follow, first one tentative paw then the other, until he was standing in the creek. Before long, he followed me round and round the shallows for at least a good half an hour. When he got comfortable, I took him where it was deeper.

When his feet could not touch, I snapped a picture of him with my phone. It is and forever will be the best picture I will ever have of Zeke. He was looking into my eyes with what seemed like blind faith or a promise to eat me in my sleep; I could not tell for sure.

I repeated that process until he learned that he could float around on his own in slow circles. When the light switched on in his head that he could swim, it was hard to get him out of the water.

Our future greenway walks now almost always had to include a swim. I took him to the big City Park that had a larger river running through it. We found a place where I would let him off the leash, and he would chase down sticks that I threw into the current. Always with his jacket on, of course.

It took a while for me to muster up the courage to take the jacket off. Just like raising kids. His world needed to get bigger.

We went on several hikes that fall and even into the winter, which was mild for Tennessee. Thanks to my boys for helping out with some much-needed training, Zeke learned a solid set of commands: Sit, Lay Down, Shake, and Wave. In addition, he learned essential hiking commands: Right, Left, Bad trail, Back up, and most importantly, Stay. All these commands were about to be put to the test.

CHAPTER 8
FINDING SUPERMAN

IT WAS LATE winter when the rains came. February became the wettest on record in Tennessee, going back to 1926, and many rivers were at their flood stage.

In the Appalachian Mountains of East Tennessee, just west of the Cumberland Plateau, there is a river that gets its name, Fall Creek, from an area where its rapids pour over an outcrop of rock and plunge more than 250 feet into a gorge below. Fall Creek Falls is the highest waterfall east of the Mississippi. An Ansel Adams photograph come to life. The stately pine, red, and white oak trees, along with maple, tulip, and hemlock, to name just a few, are the backdrop to its rugged beauty, dotted with streams, gorges, cascades, and the famed Fall Creek Falls. The rocky path that runs alongside is a challenging, muddy, and magnificent hike that ends with a 300-foot vertical climb from its base to its crest, and that is where we were going.

We got an early start with our gear. The rain had poured for days, but the morning had dawned bright, icy cold, and clear. We got on our way to see not just any waterfall but THE mother of all waterfalls. With luck, we were going to master the water hike.

The idea was to see if Zeke could follow his commands amid torrential distractions and to record some great GoPro footage for posterity.

Ready and set in his spiffy new bright red Palisades backpack, Zeke carried about twenty pounds of gear, including his water, food, bowl, and med kit. He began to pace the backseat after an hour of driving. I rolled the window down for him, and he went the rest of the way with his head and shoulders out of the car, inhaling and snorting in the freezing wind.

When we got off the I-40 Interstate and onto 111 Highway headed to the falls, my mind went back in time to my first visit to this place.

I remember waking up on the floorboard in the back of our Studebaker and climbing over the front seat to sit between my dad and my brother. The headlight beams of the old car were at a sharp angle to the road as we rounded another curve; the lights illuminated the trees exposing black chasms where the monsters were hiding. It was the fall of 1962, and I was six years old. Dad, a traveling pharmaceutical salesman who was usually gone a lot, would sometimes come home and throw some supplies in the car and take us on an adventure, or a "benture," as he called it. At the time, the only waterfalls I had ever seen were in a jungle in a Tarzan movie. So, to me, this was the jungle, and we were going camping, whatever that was.

Dad had strapped two cans of chili to the engine block of the car before we left the house to provide us a hot dinner when we got to where we were going.

If you have seen the old reruns of the *Andy Griffith Show*, you have already met my dad. Sporting a high forehead, with a wayward tumble of wavy, butternut hair and a wide, welcoming grin, he had Andy's sturdy build and folksy demeanor; guitar and all. Standing exactly six feet tall, tipping the scale at around 200 pounds, I thought he could move mountains. He could be the life of the party but, in later years, chose to stay more in the background, quietly guiding me through the chaos of growing into adulthood. Always encouraging, with a penchant for made-up words and a wealth of stories worthy of a porch and a beer, he chose to be a square peg in almost every round hole he found himself in and showed me that being different was OK.

That night in Tarzan's Jungle, I remember Dad showing us his pistol, his "Saturday Night Special," that he would use should we encounter wild animals.

I remember him pulling the massive canvas tent out of the trunk and setting it up in the headlights. I remember him breaking big sticks with his knees and starting the campfire with gasoline which initially lit up our whole campsite before dying down to a flame.

I remember screams waking me up in the middle of the night and him calmly telling me it was only a bobcat.

I remember it raining and him telling me not to touch the side of the tent, or it would leak.

I remember hiking to the waterfall in light rain, the water coming down in slow motion where some of it would billow up and not make it to the bottom, forming a mist and disappearing before it got there.

The park was quite primitive back then, and the only way to the bottom of the falls was straight down the wet rock with only a cable to hold on to. I remember Dad telling me to hold on to the cable or I would fall. I remember the bottom looking like it was miles away and the thundering sound when we got there.

I remember that when it was all over, my dad towered over me, picked me up, and somersaulted me onto his shoulders as somebody snapped a picture of me up there grinning like Superman. He would always ask after one of these *bentures*, "Well, son, did you have a day?"

THE FALLS WERE heavier than I had ever seen them. The river had overfilled its basin, and an angry cascade of water spread and bowed out, traveling over itself in twisted layers before crashing far below in a thunderous caldron of mist. This final explosion of water almost concealed the lower third of the spectacle, leaving an icy sugar-coated bowl at the bottom framed by a thick rainbow.

Zeke and I were the only witnesses at the overlook, both staring at the dangerous descent with the same expression of: *Should we be doing this?*

I took us up along the top of the falls, passing along a horseshoe bend where we crossed two rivers. The first crossing was over Piney Creek which was usually a trickle of water, but today a ravaging rampage that licked the undersides of our wooden bridge. The second bridge went over Fall Creek itself, and when we got there, it looked like a no-go. This bridge was being pummeled by rapids, with one end disappearing under white-capped waves.

When we got closer, I inspected it. I stood on the end of the bridge, which was still over land, holding the sides as I bounced up and down. I have seen bridges that are washed out, and usually, they do so after rotting over time; this one seemed new and sturdy enough, so I proceeded slowly with Zeke close behind me on his leash. When we got to near the middle, I could feel the wood buckle and thump against the angry current. I looked to my right for approaching debris, then glanced over to my left to check the riverbanks for clutch holds. If we fell in, it would be a thirty-second joyride in the freezing water before being spat out the top of the falls.

Another few careful steps and I was almost to the waves which were spilling over the planks of the bridge. I reached down, pulled off Zeke's luggage, and looped his leash under his belly around his back nice and tight, so I could hang on to him if he bailed on me. I slung his backpack around my neck and clutched onto the left-side rail; gripping the leash I instructed Zeke to stay. Slowly unspooling his leash as I went, I managed to get through the waves to the other side. Now it was Zeke's turn.

In a sitting position I placed both my feet against a facing rock that was about twenty feet between me and Zeke. Then I brought the leash up tight against my chest and yelled at him through the roar of the river, "THIS WAY! THIS WAY!!"

He started to dance side to side to test his bearings. Then squinted his eyes, holding his head up as high as he could, and entered the blast. He made it almost to the end when he was swept off the bridge and into the raging torrent. Facing upriver, Zeke swam for all he was worth but was going backward at the speed of the current. With a firm grip on the leash, I braced the rock and reeled him in like a tarpon. I could see two eyes and a nose, then more as he made it onto the bank. When he got his legs beneath him, I ran over, knelt down, and hugged his face, "GOOD BOY! GOOD BOY! Now wasn't that fun?"

His head did a half-turn before he shook his whole body from nose to whip like a slow propeller. His tail started wagging like a crazy metronome. He looked at me with bright eyes and a glow as if to say, "YEAH! Let's do that again!" I rubbed him up and down with my jacket and tried to dry him off as much as possible. Then I reached in his backpack and got the GoPro. I put in its three-legged stand and set the timer. I trotted back and had Zeke face the lens, and we snapped a picture right beside the river bridge. Then put it back in its waterproof case and slipped the luggage back on Zeke, and we were off.

Getting to the base of the falls was tricky. The steep winding path was strewn with boulders that got slicker as we neared the bottom of the cliff. The last hundred yards, I almost slid off the edge but held onto the leash, letting it go slack and yelling for Zeke to "STAY!"

Zeke stood motionless as I inched back up the rock ledge. When I got close to him, I motioned for him to go ahead. He continued down until he came to the end of his leash when I shouted, "ZEKE STOP. SIT!" Which caused him to sit down slowly and begrudgingly. It flashed across my mind right then that the last time I had yelled those commands, Zeke had gotten mauled. I passed him and continued inching down again while he stayed motionless and provided the anchor. That is the way we made it all the way to the flat at the bottom of the cliff, all in one piece.

The scene before us was surreal. The trees were winter barren having been tortured by the demonic winds from the falls, and their forfeited limbs on the ground littered the near-colorless moonscape. Both sky and ground were varying shades of grey.

The plunge pool ahead was completely covered by a towering wall of moving mist. We were not even that close to the falls yet, and I had to turn my cap around. Coated in spray, we continued through the loud roaring curtain of fog, carefully moving forward, leaning into the wall to keep our footing. And then there it was, the thundering plunge pool behind the shroud of mist that we had seen from the overlook. We were in a windstorm of frigid back-spray from what appeared to be a controlled tornado of water. Communication was impossible between us. We arrived at the limit of our ingress and had to stop, not for solid but for liquid. We stood and stared for minutes in awe. I could feel the spray freezing on my face but could not look away. Zeke was squinting and trying his best to shake with his backpack on. The moment would prove to be forever etched in my memory. Unforgettable.

After a while, we made our way back to the parking lot, doing everything in reverse. I would motion for Zeke to head back up the path to the end of his leash, then I would inch up the iced rocks, and we would do it again until we made it back off the cliff and back on the trail.

On our way out of the parking lot, I saw rangers setting up roadblocks.

They were shutting down the area because of the dangers we had already faced.

Stretched the length of the backseat, Zeke slept the whole way home with his head on his backpack.

That night, after searching through hundreds of old photographs, I found the picture of me on my father's shoulders at the falls that had been taken so long ago. I compared it to the GoPro version of Zeke and me at the river. If you ignored the grey hair and wrinkles, you would be looking at two identical six-year-old boys with the same Superman grin.

"It was good to be with you again, Dad. And yeah, we had us a day."

CHAPTER 9
TRADING PHILOSOPHIES

WORK SUCKED. I had already tried once to retire when I was age fifty. That did not pay very well; kids, dogs, and divorce were all expensive, so once again, I trudged back to a swanky bank office. I was a financial advisor who hated money, more comfortable playing darts with a guy who repossessed cars for a living, swigging stout whiskey shots, and talking about life, than attending a fancy party in a stiff penguin suit.

Most of my clients were rich, but not many were wealthy. The ones that were wealthy had two nickels in their pocket that they did not need, and that had nothing to do with being rich.

Being raised mostly in the country, the city used to fascinate me. Nashville was more of an oddity, really. Tall, old-timey, western-style Victorian architecture dating back to the 1800s housed saloons and stores with creaky floors and polished wooden counters. Back in the 1960s, we did not have big malls or the Internet, and Mom would take us there to go shopping. I remember concrete parking garages with attendants that would ride moving cable ladders and disappear through tiny holes in the roof to retrieve our car, multi-storied shops where we rode wobbly elevators driven by old men who sat beside us on padded chairs, the smell of freshly roasted peanuts in the old arcade that stretched under a cathedral glass roof, and eating in dress shop delicatessens.

At Christmastime, the toys were stacked high in shop windows. Dad would lift me up over the candy racks to watch the sprawling electric train displays laid out for the kids. It seemed like the city existed solely for our commerce. Later, its boundary ended with the last string of traffic lights as we drove the curvy two-lane roads that led back to the rolling green hills of home.

GOING TO THE city was a necessity if you wanted the nice stuff. I could not imagine ever living there or even working there. That was then, and now I was tied to it with a short leash. I had no choice but to go to it and forage like the coyote to secure my next meal.

My career path had resembled a steel ball through a Japanese pachinko machine. I had built up a sizable number of clients by the end of 2006. Then went sideways with a new manager I did not like, and eventually, I let him buy me out. It was easy living for the next few years, but the recession of 2009, kids in private schools, college expenses, and Mom's healthcare would all take a toll on my pocketbook. I had gambled and took an insurance job that ended up paying buckets of money until being sold off a couple years later, then landed at a tiny bank as a financial advisor on the platform until, finally, in the summer of 2018, a major bank had given me a shot at a wealth advisor with access to its rich customers that paraded through the lobby.

It had taken me a few months to ramp up, and I was determined to make it work if I could. I was given a two-year salary; then, I would be on straight commission. This was my final chance at being a big shot with a decent retirement.

My swanky office was on the bottom floor of a modern tower in the epicenter of downtown Nashville, where parking per day was as expensive as eighteen holes of golf at the local public course. On average, a hundred people were moving to Nashville to live every twenty-four hours. Property taxes had increased thirty-four percent overnight for everybody in the county. During the first Stanley Cup playoffs, over 50,000 had to watch it on four Megatrons set up in the streets because there was not enough room to fit them in the hockey stadium.

My little bungalow had sextupled in value with tall skinnies going up all around, that is what we called the remodeled Victorian bungalows that were regularly being torn down along with all their charm then built up high and wide within an inch of their property line, taking advantage of the sky-rising property values. It was as if all of America had discovered our beautiful and vibrant city and countryside all at once. It soon became typical to find a note taped to my front door from realtors and the newly arrived eager to buy.

Downtown had become a maze of party buses, golf carts, hot rods, horse-drawn carriages, Uber drivers, tourist vans, motorcycle cops, and drunk ladies singing at the top of their lungs on wagons pulled by farm tractors. And that was on a Tuesday.

My daily commute was a combination of cussing mixed with prayer through an all-out, no-holds-barred bumper car race to the safety of the building garage. The goals given to me were twenty calls a day, twenty appointments per week to bring in one million dollars in assets a month to keep management off my back. Then I would limp home to do it all again.

Except I was not doing it. My numbers were horrible. I might have looked like a big shot, but I was burnt out. Washed up. I could barely afford parking. My salary was only going to last until June. And although I had some savings, I was near to being priced out of my own neighborhood.

Coming into the lobby, I got a few nods from the white shirts, walked down the long corridor of doors, and found mine. As soon as I unlocked it the phone was ringing.

"Good morning." It was my boss, and he sounded blunt and to the point. It wasn't as bad as it could have been; he said he wanted to schedule a one-on-one phone meeting every two weeks with me and wanted me to send him a list of every activity I had accomplished for the week. It was to include a day-by-day description, and he wanted it each week by the end of the day on Friday. He asked me if I had a problem with it.

I replied, "No. No sir."

Then the phone clicked off. I leaned my elbows on my desk and buried my face in my hands.

I heard my door open.

"Knock, knock." It was Linda, my assistant.

She opened the door herself. "Good *morning*," she sang.

"Do you have to be so cheerful?" I asked.

"Let me guess. You either got hit by a truck, or you've already talked to Frank."

Soberly, I replied, "He put me on an action plan."

Cheerily, she said, "I brought you some coffee."

I mimicked her cheeriness, "Great. I'll put that in my action plan!"

Linda put the coffee on my desk.

"I'll drop by later if I need cheering up," she said as she closed the door behind her.

I took my head out of my hands and logged into my computer to look at my emails.

There were several, mainly junk.

Then I spotted a nasty one from compliance. Apparently, I had 'liked' and commented on an article on social media, which was a compliance no-no. I was given a written warning in the email, as it had been my second offense in a year, and my debriefing, or 'slap on the wrist,' had already been scheduled and was on my calendar.

"Bastards," I grumbled.

I worked in perhaps the most regulated and micromanaged world that exists. The compliance hawks watched and monitored everything I did, which was necessary for the world we lived in now but counter to who I was. I was an old-fashioned banker who liked to get to know the folks who trusted me to steward their future means. I was 'a story over a martini and a steak' kinda guy in a business that now disallowed any sort of fraternizing that involved real human interaction. It was like every letter, every email that I sent out, every comment I made on social media was evidence to use against me in a lawsuit. I could not let out a sneeze without getting an email: *Gesundheit!*

I had not been in the office twenty minutes and was already itching to get lost on a hill with Zeke. I called up a few usual prospects and had some conversations but no buyers. At least I could log those as activities.

Now the pressure was on; my income runway was getting short. I spent the next two hours with my screen angled right in front of me and away from the door. I searched the job market, and there were plenty of 'em, but not for a sixty-something-year-old advisor with no clients. I started searching for other jobs that I might be good at; there were entry-level jobs, but I was too old for that. I slurped the last of my coffee down and went to lunch. At least I had a salary for the next few months. Surely, I could find something by then.

By the end of the day, I had logged my activities. Half were real, the others I just made up. When I got home, Zeke was waiting. He wagged his tail slowly, and I got his leash. Those winter days were short, and it was already dark. We loped around outside awhile until he got bored; my heart was just not in it; all I could do was ponder my current predicament.

The next morning, after some looking around on the computer, I had found the phone number of someone much more interesting to talk to than the prospects that would not take my calls. I had not talked to Randy in over fifteen years.

Randy, an old high school buddy of mine, had a farm on the outskirts of town. One of the smartest kids in school, but with zero ambition, Randy had inherited plenty of money, and chose to live the quiet life alone on his farm.

Back in our school days, we had gotten into plenty of trouble together. He had worn his hair below his shoulders and sported a man-worthy mustache that curled down his mouth to his chin. Always in baggy shirts and jeans, he kept a derringer in his boot. He was the only son of a pair of misfit parents. His dad had a big-time job somewhere and was barely in the picture without a shouting match, and his mother could talk the balls off a brass monkey. Their sprawling ranch house hung on the edge of a cliff high over the Cumberland River with a dirty swimming pool decorated by algae-covered statues. Inside was a disorganized, dark, and dusty Smithsonian Museum with exotic treasures stacked so high it was impossible to appreciate them individually. There were books, skulls, animals with glass eyes gazing lifelessly, and antique dolls with teeth. It was like Stephen King's playhouse.

Happy to hear from me, Randy invited me to come over to have a few beers. I buzzed Linda that I would be out of pocket tomorrow as I was courting a big prospect. Then I smiled. I was about to play hooky.

I brought Zeke along, and we took him on a stroll around his land. It was 250 acres of mostly tall grass fields with a tree-lined river, a lake, a barn, and an old farmhouse, his 'bunker.'

We talked about old times, The Beatles, motorcycles, and the life choices we had made. I asked him if he was happy. He said after he bought the farm, he never looked back. He said he felt like John Lennon in grade school. I asked what he meant by that. He replied, "Well, when Lennon was in grade school, his first homework assignment was to write what he wanted to be in life. He just wrote down the word, Happy. They told him he didn't understand the assignment; he told 'em they didn't understand life."

I had not been to his farm in years but spotted an old rusty bike he had in the barn; in the same place I had last seen it years before.

"Hah! You still got the Green," I said as I quickly went over to inspect it.

When I had first spotted this bike, it was many years ago; it seemed like yesterday ...

2003

IT WAS THE summer of 2003 on a hot day in June. Randy and I shared many things, including our love for motorcycles, and he had the money to buy them. I heard his phone ring while I was inspecting one of his most recent purchases, an old mint condition 1980 Husqvarna CR250 on its pegs with the keys dangling from the ignition.

Randy held the phone to his chest and bellowed across the barn, "Why don't you take that and jump the creek with it."

I hesitated, "Are you sure I can get across?"

He motioned out the barn, nodded his head, and went back to his caller.

It had been a while, but I was familiar with this bike. I flicked the key to the ignition mark, straddled the seat, got my whole foot on the kickstart. Then I raised up and bounced on the kick a few times until it rattled into life like a 250cc weed eater. Blue smoke and all.

I backed it up and took off over the field, bouncing on the dirt and feeling like a kid. When I saw the creek, it looked deep as I slowly crept up to the edge. I turned the bike around to give myself some more room. I backed it up 100 feet, then revved on the throttle a few times, then let out the clutch and gave it all she had.

I was doing at least thirty when I hit the water. The bike immediately dove down under me as I went over the handlebars and landed with a big splash. I held on to the handlebars as long as I could until we were both underwater. The engine stayed running for a few seconds and was belching bubbles of smoke with each "*bloop, bloop, bloop,*" and finally stopped.

It took a few minutes of struggle, but I managed to fish the bike out of the creek. I pulled my helmet off and was soaked, and so was the poor bike. Randy had seen and heard the commotion and was slowly walking toward my direction with a smirk on his face, looking at the ground and shaking his head, laughing at my predicament.

When he got close, I expressed my frustration, "I thought you said I could cross it!"

Randy said, "This ain't the creek."

I sputtered, "Oh. My bad."

We finally got the bike started again, walked it to the house, and sat under an oak tree drinking beer in the bright sun until my clothes had dried off. We talked about old times and the bikes we had when we were in school. He said he had something to show me in the shed.

If you could have your pick of all the iconic antique sports bikes of the seventies decade, it was the H2. The Kawasaki H2 Mach IV was commonly referred to as the "Widowmaker," and he had two in his shed, a green one and a purple one.

With three coffee can-sized cylinders that accommodated a 750cc two-stroke engine, it would blow your hair back. It was the fastest bike on the road and could finish a quarter-mile from a standing start in twelve seconds. It was faster because of its large two-cycle engine. It may have leaked, smoked, and been problematic, but a two-stroke could do twice as much work as a four-stroke in the same amount of time, and it ran and sounded like a screaming, scalded dog. It was heavily modified in later years mainly for emission standards and because it was just plain dangerous.

I chose the purple and Randy the green, we hopped on each, and in a few seconds, we were tearing off together like we did in high school.

Randy knew the way, so I followed close to his taillight. Soon we were riding around a ribbon of roads like two over-the-hill James Deans on steroids, connected to each other by an invisible bungee cord. I trusted Randy as he was the best rider I knew. I was following so close that I was watching him instead of the road. Whatever was in front of us was a quick dash through the double yeller and in the rear-view seconds later. If a squirrel had darted out and caught our tires, we would have both been sent to the limestone ledges beside us like bugs on a windshield. This all might seem insane until you try it. You cannot feel this way without experiencing the rush of rocketing over winding country roads while hearing the high-pitched two-strokes.

We got so fast on the straight highways that when we relaxed the throttles, the steering damper would wobble till we downshifted to lean into another bank. No ABS brakes back in those days; you had to rely on the engine's torque to keep from skidding. God was I *so* not at the office.

After thirty miles and lunch at a general store, it was getting late, and we were ready to go back. We rode now at a slower pace; we were not kids anymore.

When we got to the farm, it was nightfall. We parked next to each other and sat down on the ground to rest a bit. I needed to go back home. Randy lit up a cigarette, then asked me if I could trade a day for anything, what would I trade it for? The bikes were leaning on their pegs with the hot exhaust pipes clicking and hissing in the cool night air.

I answered immediately, "I'll trade my car for the purple!"

He laughed so much I thought he would choke, "You got yourself a deal, partner."

I got on the purple H2, reached in my pocket, pitched him my car keys, and bounced on the kickstart. The bike smoked and revved an angry whine.

Randy yelled out, "Just watch it cause that headlight needs adjustin'."

"Don't worry." I yelled back, "I'll be on the interstate before you can find the wrenches!"

I sped off down the long driveway of the farm, throwing up gravel and dirt, and turned onto the road at the end. The maladjusted headlight pointed at a steep angle up in the night sky, but I could still see the road well enough. I twisted the throttle and slid back in the seat from the rush of the two-stroke. I was in the sweet spot of third gear when the road ahead of me vanished to the left. In a split second, I knew I was gone.

I leaned the bike to the left and turned the handlebars to the right to lay it down and minimize impact. The bike slid for a few yards into the woods and smacked into a low and hidden drainage ditch, high-siding me and the bike into the air. I flew over the handlebars and hit a thick snarl of kudzu vines in a grove of trees. The kudzu provided a cushioned landing for me, and it felt like I had been smacked into a mattress at 40 mph. I lay there for a while and attempted to reorient myself, checking for major breaks, and realized I was wearing full coverage, everything Kevlar: jacket, jeans, gloves, helmet, boots, and thought I had done pretty good. I was underneath the kudzu thicket, and the totaled bike was on top of me, still groaning in a low idle. I reached back, grabbed some kudzu for leverage, and pulled myself out from under the red-hot pipes. Soon I saw the headlights of a vehicle as it veered in my lane and screeched to a stop just feet from my head. The car was mine.

The door slammed, and I heard footsteps.

"You ok?" Randy was running to my side.

I managed to squeak out, "I've fallen down, and I can't get up."

I was laughing and shaking and pretending. I still did not know if any bones had been shattered. The motorcycle gods had smiled on me again. As I surveyed the area a few days later, I realized that only an owl could have missed as many trees as I did that night.

I went in to work the next day, limping with a bruise from my lower chest all the way over my shoulder and down my back. My arm was in a sling but thankfully nothing was broken but my pride.

My assistant at the time looked me up and down, "You look awful!!"

I replied, "This is nothin'. You oughta see the client."

"What really happened?" she asked.

"Motorcycle wreck," I replied.

"You have a motorcycle?" Incredulous, she raised her eyebrows.

I sat down gingerly, adjusted my big shot self at my desk, and replied, "Not anymore."

ZEKE WAS ASLEEP on the barn floor beside the rusty bike of the kudzu incident. I was sipping on a cold Bud. Randy had a glowing joint in his mouth, his cap on backward.

"I'm still sorry about that bike," I said, nodding over to the old green, rusty H2.

His face lit up in a wide grin, "I can still 'member yer face, man. You looked like the creature from the kudzu crawling outta there."

He slapped a knee, laughing out loud, almost falling out of his chair. I gave him the finger and leaned back in my chair.

Wiping the tears from his face, he choked out, "So you workin' at a bank, huh? What's that like?"

How could I describe it?

I replied, "It's like waking up in the morning and wishin' the day was over."

As I sipped on my beer, Randy, slightly buzzed and feeling good, started to philosophize, "I been around some people who got money. Seemed like they was always talkin' 'bout it too. Always showing themselves off."

He took another toke on the blunt, inhaling deeply and blowing out a stream of smoke, "My folks were rich. But I never been much in a bank."

Growing up, Randy had his own small trailer where he lived parked just outside of the garage of his parents' house. It was messy with experiments all around and always full of smoke. Half-built contraptions lay under a spaghetti of wires, with a chemistry set complete with distillation apparatus butted against a small, musty mattress where he slept. At sixteen, he had an amateur's understanding of astronomy, quantum physics, philosophy, and history. He once read an entire trigonometry textbook in a single night for fun. But even so, he steadfastly refused to use any other language but countrified English, which, to me, only enhanced his magnetism.

I introduced him to my family, and he was taken in, mesmerized by my happy, loving home. He would often come over and sleep on the floor beside my bed. Of course, things were not as innocent as they seemed to Mom and Dad. I had a Honda 350 twin motorcycle hidden under a brush pile in a ditch and would often sneak out my window at midnight and tear through the streets with Randy on his H2. We regularly smoked dope in his orange Camero in my driveway listening to Pink Floyd on an eight-track while we traded philosophies.

"Your folks were nice," I mused.

"Yeah, I got along with my folks just fine. But I seen money and what it done to people. After my folks died, I just took the money they give me and stuck it in this piece 'a land. That way, I can't spend none of it, but I can walk all over it every day. Money didn't change me one damned bit."

It was good to see Randy. After one long goodbye hug and a slap on the back, we promised each other we would stay in touch. I drove away, back to the city and my job.

I dreaded the next day of work but decided to try to bring in some good prospects. And I would be there earlier than usual this time. As Dad would say: "If you gotta swallow a frog, don't stare at it too long."

CHAPTER 10

MY FATHER'S GIFTS

I HAD FINALLY made it to Friday afternoon and was finishing my activity list. Albeit the finished report contained some flat-out lies, during the past week I had acquired some decent prospects and set a number of appointments. It is amazing what can happen if you do some work. I emailed it to my boss just short of the five o'clock deadline and turned everything off.

The traffic was a crawl, and it took thirty minutes just to make the six miles back to my house; my mind was already ten thousand miles away back to my home, the home where I came from.

My roots are anchored deep in the rich red clay of West Tennessee, or "God's country," as Dad would say. Both my parents had been born in farmhouses. And when I say, "born in farmhouses," I mean that literally, as the doctor made house calls back then. Their two respective farmhouses were located on farms that abutted one another, bordered only by land and a long barbed-wire fence. That is how small and tight my family upbringing would be. Growing up as a kid surrounded by hundreds of kinfolks, I thought everybody was supposed to have grandparents who lived next door to each other, and I felt sorry for the kids who didn't.

I had a Deerfield sixteen-gauge shotgun and was hunting squirrels and quail at twelve years old. The woods and the land we walked on were all ours. When it got cold in the fall of the year, we would look for rabbit tobacco; a plant about three feet tall, with silvery green leaves and yellowish aromatic buds. My father showed me how to smoke these buds, crushing and rolling them into small blunts with brown paper from old grocery bags, then carefully lighting the end. He explained the Indians believed it had medicinal qualities. For us, it was just fun.

Everything we ate had either been grown or raised, and the 'extry,' that which was left over was sold at the courthouse square or the local farmer's market in town. The money was used to buy supplies, feed, and anything else we were not able to grow, fix or make ourselves.

I never thought I was poor growing up as a kid. We always had plenty. When I would get around rich kids, I was never jealous. It wasn't until I grew up that I realized that pretty girls had rather ride around in a shiny new sports car than sit at a red light in a rusty old Vega with a hand-painted racing stripe down the side. I decided then to oblige them by going into big money finance.

Sunrise woke us up early. It was Saturday. I stumbled out of bed, made some coffee, and poured through the lists of jobs that were available on the computer job sites. I scoured them all: LinkedIn, Career Builder, Indeed, GlassDoor, every job that I felt suitable for. By the end of an hour, I had filled out sixteen job applications. The effort had proved to be more exhausting than working at the office, but I had to throw out an SOS, as the proverbial boat was sinking fast.

Head in hands again, I thought of Dad. Thinking of dad had always made me feel better in times like these. I sure as heck did not learn about money-rich from my dad. Three years before I was born, he had moved his family: my mom and my brother to the big city of Nashville. By the time I was six years old he was divisional manager of his pharmaceutical company but was still more comfortable eating sardines out of a can than eating mahi-mahi in a swanky restaurant. He stayed gone a lot. Until one day in 1962, when he told my mom that he did not want to miss seeing us kids grow up and just up and quit his job.

It took me a very selfishly long time before I started to appreciate that. Once, I asked him how he could have afforded to do such a thing.

His answer was, "Couldn't afford not to. That weren't no job. My job was you and your brother." There was nothing but straight line in his voice. He was just stating a fact.

A quiet listener, he was the only person who could finish my sentences. His greatest advice came from under his breath.

When I would ask him about career choices, he would tell me, "Just make sure it ain't work, son."

When I asked him about women, he would say, "Pick you out an ugly one, son. They'll treat you better."

For four years during World War II, he proudly served as an aircraft mechanic onboard the Antietam, a carrier in the South Pacific. As he got older, he would talk more and more about the war, and I now regret that I had not written down every single word. He smiled a lot, was transparent and truthful, a sublimely honorable and capable man.

In order to settle my divorce in 1995, the decree mandated payment of a tremendous sum that I couldn't afford. My dad borrowed all he could and paid it.

It took me six years, but I paid him back without interest in 2001. Before I handed him the check, I asked him how he could have taken such a chance at his age by risking his retirement on me.

He answered matter-of-factly with a wink and a grin, "That's my job, son."

He became less talkative in his later years, resorting to staying on the old farm for days at a time occupying the old cabin of his childhood, which decayed around him, sharing only the company of a cellphone and five or more house cats.

Often, we would stay up late, watch old war movies, and hold deep conversations about life. With a GED, he was mostly self-taught, but I never caught up to his intellect or intuitiveness. During times that I struggled, he would look into my eyes and tell me what I was thinking. He let me solve my own problems even as he gently led me to the right conclusion, then would smile and nod when I got it right.

When he was diagnosed with cancer in 2003, I was there with him by his hospital bed most every night. One night I told him somberly that he had no idea how much I wished it were me on that bed instead of him. He opened his eyes slightly and gave me a grin, "Yer times a-comin', son. Ain't no use in a-goin' thru it twice."

On a June morning in 2004, I got a call. It was Dad on the phone. He had randomly called just to see how I was *Frognosticating*? (That was his word for, "How is life treating you?").

We talked for several minutes, and at the end of our conversation, I told him that I loved him. That afternoon, while walking out of a Food Lion with a sack of groceries, he had a massive heart attack.

My brother and I helped carry Dad in a flag-draped casket and laid him to rest a few miles from the old farm. He may have been the sincerest listener I ever knew, but since we closed the lid on that casket, he ain't shut up yet.

CHAPTER 11

PONDERING THE LEASH

TWO LARGE SPIDERS hung from the brim of my cap and dangled in front of me. After carefully brushing them off with my free hand, I searched for a good spider stick. Zeke and I were in the hinterlands of Kentucky about seven miles or so from the car. My only goals were to free my mind from work and the city and lose cellphone service as quickly as possible.

It was the fall of 2019, and the trees were dropping their leaves, ablaze with color. The path ahead was straight and wide but riddled with webs. Spiders live for about a year, so late in the year, they get big. On this trip I saw some monsters. We had never hiked this region and were looking forward to seeing new terrain.

Underneath our feet lay the longest cavernous system on Earth. This Mammoth Cave State Park has a remote area that is accessible by crossing Green River on a two-car cable ferry. It has no amenities, and a permit is required to camp. The sites are placed miles apart, so we were assured of no human interaction for the next two days. Zeke and I were good with that. I was getting to like his world better than mine anyway.

It had been a hot summer followed by a dry, warm fall. In contrast to the winter and spring of that year, we were in a drought. I had passed many dry riverbeds and was getting a bit uneasy. I had been lost on a few trails in my lifetime. It is very disheartening and scary when you have been walking on your return trip for miles, only to discover you are in a different and unseen territory. There is food all around you but no substitute for water.

Lost hikers have starved lying within feet of a buffet of plentiful food sources. The ability to identify edible plants, insects, and saprophytes can separate one from life or death in dire circumstances. I've made it a hobby to test myself, snapping pictures of live subjects on tree bark, guessing its name, and googling it when I got home for accuracy. If a deer has chewed on the plants or mushrooms, for instance, it is usually a good sign that the species is not poisonous. If unknown, you can ingest a small bite and wait for signs. It might make you a trifle sick, but you will not die from eating a tiny bit. There are five wild mushrooms I can identify. The easiest of these is *Laetiporus sulphureus*, a bright orange shelf mushroom that grows horizontally from a tree, which can be spotted at a great distance away. It is full of nutrition and delicious when boiled, hence its nickname, 'Chicken of the woods.' Edible plants are plentiful enough, animals are free for the taking, and insects are quite nourishing. However, without water, you will be dead in a few days, even with a belly full of bugs.

The terrain was rocky, as you would expect a cavernous area to be. Through the years, the limestone had given way through water erosion, and occasionally we would find a hole large enough to enter in the side of a rock ledge, but I'm not much of a caver. I like to be out in the nice and open. The temperature inside a significant cave system in Tennessee and Kentucky is a constant fifty-five to sixty degrees Fahrenheit. I have hiked in cavernous areas and experienced a sudden ten-degree temperature change due to the invisible open mouths of caves in the vicinity. That can come in handy if you are in need of shelter or to cool down in extreme heat; even in late fall, the temps could easily soar into the nineties.

My idea of fun, however, is not to be in a closed dark dungeon of a cave trying to find my way out again. It reminded me too much of the office.

Over the last two years, Zeke had bulked up from our hiking and, at almost four years old, had finally stopped growing. On any given day, he could range from 100 to 110 pounds. Lean, strong, and handsome, his short black hair made him gleam in the sun like a seal. His wishbone-shaped face was always curious. Zeke looked up at me, his eyes bright. He had lost the dull greyness of depression that had persisted for so long after his mauling. He tilted his head as he loped along with his backpack, looking to me for cues.

I've been hiking alone ever since I was a young kid. My grandfather taught me how to shoot, and I learned from him as I watched him live off the land, a matter-of-fact, salt-of-the-earth pioneer.

Edgar Rhodes was as tall and rugged as the ancient oak trees that dotted the dirt farm he tilled. With crooked leather hands, he forged a life out of seventy acres in West Tennessee, helped only by a couple of mules, a crosscut saw, and a Bible. To us kids, he was a history book that smoked a pipe. He was lean, tanned, and fairly weathered by the time I first formed memories of him. His grey hair was short and stood straight up out of his head. He wore black, thick-framed glasses, overalls, and a straw pith helmet that shielded his deeply furrowed brow and sharp green eyes that could stare down a bull. His voice was baritone and filled with so many old colloquialisms that his sagacity was barely understood by those who lived the easy life in the city. A voice that was soothing and guiding. A strong voice that clearly knew good from bad and right from wrong.

My childhood memories of his farm are of a much simpler time, of sitting on a summer day in a porch swing with a fly swatter in one hand, a twelve-cent comic book in the other, feeling the breeze from the kitchen window fan and hearing the hum of granddaddy's tractor, of smelling the combination of chicken frying on the stove, cornbread sticks in the oven, and pipe tobacco, all rolled into one. A handout of Juicy Fruit gum, a can of Leo peppermints, and long stick matches were always within reach. Taking baths in a washtub, the cold outhouse in the winter, eating fresh-caught fish or frogs from the pond, drinking the cold well water, and rabbit hunting with Rusty, his copper-colored farm dog.

Zeke had slowed his pace; his heavy pant let me know he was thirsty. I motioned for him to keep going, and he took off, leading me up the trail.

Dogs are masters in the study of habits and cues. I can ask Zeke if he wants to go for a ride by just my mouth forming the word "Go" and jingling my keys. I never ask him to do something I do not think he is ready to do, and I also have never ever lied to him. I have too much invested in his trust. And right now, he was trusting me to find us some water.

After a mile of seeing no other animals, I noticed a big rat snake sunning itself, uncoiled on a rock. Of the many snakes in Tennessee and Kentucky, only four are poisonous: cottonmouth, copperhead, timber rattlesnake, and the pygmy rattlesnake. My son and I once had to carefully tiptoe a trek pole's length around an angry timber rattler, but since that incident, most of the snakes I have encountered have been the non-venomous variety. Rat snakes are plentiful, and young ones can be confused with the similarly banded, extremely poisonous cottonmouth. The adult rat snake is much darker and commonly reaches five to seven feet in length. This one was in the middle, about as long as the dog that loped by me in my shadow. No snake is worth approaching when coiled, as it is prepared to strike. But, as with the snake I was now studying, being uncoiled usually means it is non-aggressive and not in a defensive mode and could be our clue to finding a water source nearby.

Sure enough, I spotted a large cavern directly under a hanging ledge in front of us.

It was wet and creepy and just what we needed. A trickle of water dripped into a small clear puddle in an otherwise dry bed. It took forever, but I managed to get five liters of precious water in the bladder and bottles I had unfolded out of my pack while Zeke explored the cave. That tiny trickle would prove to be the only water source we saw on the whole eighteen-mile trip. A few hours later, we were setting up camp.

At our site, I hitched Zeke up to a lone metal post that had hangers and carefully hung the bladder of water without spilling a drop.

The basic structure of our light backpacker's tent consisted of a floor, a see-through mesh above it with a zippered door and window openings, held up by flexible poles. The roof, or 'fly' gave privacy and protection from the weather. This night was mild, so I left off the fly.

I built a big fire, as this time of year the temperature can turn quickly, and started supper. I poured some boiling water over something that was supposed to be beef stroganoff and sat down to eat. After Zeke's dogfight, I had resorted to buying his food at a local dog boutique in an effort to get him to eat. Now he was happily crunching on a holistic salmon likely of a better quality than the space food I was wolfing down. Definitely more expensive.

There were at least a million stars. I could see the Milky Way winding its swath. I noticed the ground in front of me was scattered with glitter, like so much broken glass in tiny pieces that shimmered in my headlamp. That was a weird phenomenon that I had never seen, so I walked over to have a look. As I examined one of the glitters closeup, I found a motionless spider with eight little eyes staring back at me. I estimated there were thousands of them. I mused that they must get few visitors and that we were their free entertainment for the night.

I had heard distant music from coyotes earlier while making the fire. It occurred to me they always sound so happy. But, in actuality, they were hunting. Hungry and communicating to the pack, they usually hunt individually, but they need to know where the others are, and the constant yipping is for that reason. It also comes in handy when making larger kills.

We were about two miles away from the Green River, where there was no trail access, and by the sound of them, they were methodically combing the hill.

We enjoyed a perfect Jack London moment. The fire with its rolling flames sputtered, hissed, and popped sparks up to tree limbs. Zeke's eyes reflected bright red from my headlamp, always with his front legs crossed. The tiny spiders provided the glitter that surrounded our little scene, and the yips every fifteen minutes from the coyotes provided the soundtrack.

I drank the bourbon from my flask. It is here in the whole of this environment where I can clearly think. I have made many permanent decisions in places like this. I inhaled another puff on my cigar and kicked the glowing embers in front of me, stirring the fire with my boot.

I thought about the path I had taken in my life. I mean, what six-year-old kid wants to grow up to be a banker?

IN THE SMOKY Mountains, there is a rock called Chimney Tops. At an altitude of 4,794 feet, it is my favorite summit. The shortest hike to it is a seven miler, and to reach it you need to spider climb another 200 feet along steep folds of smooth metamorphic stone, stacked high like teetering pancakes on a plate, creating natural hand and footholds. You are rewarded at the top with a three-sixty vista of the park, which covers two states. It is a great place to watch a sunset as long you do not mind the bats flying by your head on the way back down. I knew every step of that trail by heart in the year 1981 because I was making that trek almost every other weekend to sit atop it and think.

I would watch an eagle drift through silent air without fear of falling to the world below it. I would marvel at how the ground creatures would hardly notice the steepness of their harsh environment. I would gaze at the sparse vegetation itself, how it would glow green and healthy through the cracks of boulders, having found enough nutrients to take root. I would note the perfect order of the colors of sunset as they changed through the twilight sky, the longer red wavelengths of light finally forced through thicker air as the sun slowly touched the horizon. Then the thin line of dusk framed with a canopy of stars. I would then climb down guided by the faint afterglow on the rock and reverse my seven miles, trudging and tripping on tree roots and listening to the blind bats fly by me in the darkness. I spent the journey back pondering my predicament in jealous envy of the life and calm serenity I had left on the rock.

That was the summer I had started back to college. So far in life, I had barely made it out of high school, totaled two cars and a motorcycle, tried welding, dropped out of college to join a band, and now I was back studying something called 'Chemical Engineering' that I had picked out of an enrollment book. I had never met a chemical engineer nor knew anything about what one did, but the book said they made good money and the girlfriend I had at the time wanted to be rich. I also knew that one quarter's worth of studying for my newfound career had been about as much fun as a three-month root canal. Neither of those relationships worked out, by the way. She ran off with a doctor, and I became an investment banker just for spite. You've heard of Magna Cum Laude? I finally graduated with a Thank-You-Lawd.

My trail through life had been cut by trial and error. I could walk for miles through desolate geyser basins and bear scat and get where I wanted to be without a hitch. But in life, there's no map; I can only look back to see the waypoints, the places I've been. Then God throws in stuff like kids and dogs just to show me that I don't really know what love is until I've been through the hell of it, then love becomes much more visible, clearer, and more unmistakable. I concluded that life was a continuous barrage of lessons, and Zeke had me in the middle of a cram course.

Back there on that rock, things just seemed so perfect. Everything fit together neat and simple up there on the top of the world. It's funny; I can remember so much about the rock on the summit and so little about the return trip. At the top was alive and sunny. Down from it, a dark mess. In a way, I don't think I ever came down from that rock. The rock, in my mind, is where I want to stay, where all is perfect. Not my life.

It was getting late, and I was out of bourbon, so I threw the rest of my cigar in the glowing embers and added a large log to light the camp up again. I checked the area for trash, careful to store all the food in dry sacks inside the tent to keep away the nighttime varmints. Minutes later, Zeke and I were laid out next to each other, listening to the crickets, and every fifteen minutes, the yip song of the coyotes. Shortly after getting comfortable, Zeke quietly rose and settled by the door. I started to call him back to my side but was too sleepy to care and promptly drifted off.

Until the sounds outside our tent woke me. "YOOOOOYIPYIPYIP!! Yeeeepyeeeep. YOOOOO!!"

How many were there?

I counted five or six in my head. My watch read 2:30 am. With the fly off we were exposed, having only the see-through net between the marauders and us; our only cover was the pitch black.

There were two on my right and maybe three on the left, and they were plenty pissed off about Zeke being in their home digs. The fact that they would attack with a still-smoking fire had me a bit unsettled.

I could hear a few loping around in the dark. I estimated they were as close as ten feet now, maybe closer. Glad I had put everything in the tent; I still had no weapon. You can fend off an animal with a backpack or a trekking pole, but a pack of coyotes in the night's blackness might prove a bit superhuman.

When two dark shadows on my right approached the door, Zeke, in a low tense crouch, deeply snarled. I fumbled in the dark, my hand grabbing the first hard thing I could find.

I clutched the GoPro, thinking to burst from the tent and scare them off. I quietly moved to get out of the sleeping bag when Zeke's snarl turned in my direction.

I turned on my headlamp, and there Zeke stood, his head making a huge hump in the top of the tent, still in an ominous crouch, his haunches not even touching the ground. He was blocking my exit. I started to move, and again, the low growl was thrown at me. Something in his stance told me he knew something I did not. I froze, sat back, and gave him the floor.

I could see the light from my headlamp casting his shadow even larger on the ground outside when suddenly, he blew out a Baskerville satanic yowl such that I had never heard, his breath steaming out in great puffs in the cold night air. The bellow resembled the loud howl of a wolf but was much deeper and spookier. He stretched it out until it ended with a tearful cry that slowly petered out, echoing in the trees around us.

Zeke stood still and motionless, blocking the door. If I tried to move from my sitting position, his eyes would quickly return to me along with a low-growl warning. I could only scan the woods with my two big golf ball-sized eyes searching for a speck of light, straining to locate and figure out how many coyotes there were now. I could still hear rustling in the tree line, their pads loping as they circled the campsite.

Zeke slowly rose on his haunches, backing up toward me; he softly growled his breaths in and out with an evil grin, coming to a stop when he stood over my legs, my face level with his body, his tail suddenly slapping my face and the sides of the tent.

Then he threw his head up and bellowed the same slow, mournful groan again with his nose in the air, and his eyes squinted closed this time. This one ended in a large growl death throe then whimpered out to a gasp. I heard a few gallops in the distance.

Then silence. Dark, heavy silence.

Who was this beast that I slept with? Who was this transformed half dog, half wolf creature I suddenly did not know or recognize? Zeke lowered his body onto my legs, making it final that he was not letting me go anywhere.

For what seemed like hours, Zeke and I waited in the blackness; the familiar song of the coyotes brought me back to the present. Their calls were off in the distance now as they continued their hunt.

Zeke turned and sniffed my face. Then he resumed his earlier position by the door, lay down, and closed his eyes.

Peering out of my sleeping bag, I whispered to him, “Thanks, buddy.”

He responded with a loud exhale, then deep breathing, which transformed into a soft snore. Our tent suddenly seemed quite small, and above the stars wrapped around the Earth, and outside the tent, the coals of the fire glowed softly, and there was a calm that abided within us.

The night sounds slowly resumed. A whippoorwill cried mournfully. A band of katydids resembled voices. The crickets joined in the rhythm. Then the frogs.

Exhausted, I drifted off into a deep, uninterrupted sleep.

By morning, the coyotes were howling again while I made breakfast. Not wanting to overstay our welcome, I packed up our gear and surrendered the hill. It was theirs anyways.

Back on the trail, while tearing through another one of eight thousand newly made dew-covered webs in front of me with my spider stick, the thought of going to work the next morning slowed my pace. I gazed in wonder at the web-ladened, tree-filled world around me. What if there were none of this? If mankind lived only in a city with all its empty artificial baubles. And then someone built a sky outside of it; how many people would rush and clamor to see it? How many would eagerly throw away their riches to live under it?

As we rounded the last trailhead on the way to the car, it struck me that if last night had happened even a year ago, and Zeke had heard the approaching mess of coyotes, would he have offered to stay in the tent between me and the door?

I thought about how he had loped around my house on that first Christmas, looking for exits, cracked doors, open fence gates, hoping to find a winning lottery ticket to escape. But last night, his leash was slack. Instead of running, he had protected me from dangers that he had once faced alone. I might be the one on his leash now instead of the other way around. Whatever the reason, we kept holding onto the leash, he and I.

CHAPTER 12
RICHNESS AND WEALTH

THE FINANCIAL WORLD, as with most other aspects of humanity, evolved quickly with technology. By the 1990s, an industry that was earlier dominated by individuals who tried to find bargain stocks by using only their wit had gone by way of the dinosaur, replaced by computers that could instantly trade with a speed that surpassed human capability. By the time the news was printed and delivered to the stockbrokers, it had already been gobbled up and digested by the 'program traders' who charged a fee for their services. They were the experienced gurus who kept eyes glued on eight monitors, deciphering the undulating human greed displaying itself in charts, graphs, and tickers, all the while eating turkey sandwiches and competing in fiber-optic length across the oceans. I, of the electric adding machine generation, could only sit back and watch.

Investment firms started spending money on personality polls, trying to understand what was going on in the heads of their clients. They found out two important things: first, the rich wanted to get richer, no surprise there. Secondly, what was surprising was that eighty-five percent of accumulated family wealth would usually disappear by the third generation. In other words, the children were squandering all the money.

One of the most brazen examples of this occurred with the Vanderbilt family. Cornelius Vanderbilt went from rags to riches and became one of the wealthiest men this country has ever produced. By building an empire of railroads and shipping fleets, he amassed a fortune. At the end of his life in 1877, he had an estate of over 105 million dollars (sixty-eight billion in today's dollars). His estate was bitterly contested by four of the children, with one committing suicide before it was all settled. After the money was distributed, it was spent on lavish parties and palatial houses with such speed and stupidity that forty-six years later, the first Vanderbilt died penniless. By 1973, there were no more millionaires left. Their money was a mindless commodity and their unearned fortune a curse. William K. Vanderbilt, a grandson of Cornelius, once said, "Inherited wealth is as fatal to my ambition as cocaine is to my mortality." But that seemed to be the cycle of the rich, and the companies that served these clients wanted to know more.

Management directed us to have longer meetings with clients to get to know them. I started calling prospects with a new list of questions designed to engage them about what made them tick. Most of the conversations were an exercise in futility, the clients preferring to stay fixated upon their quantification and measure of opulence. And although the number of houses and cars they had accumulated may have been interesting at first, I was far more interested in their life stories — what were their dreams and ambitions, who would they die for, how did they get all this money? — that was more interesting than how many Rolexes they owned; for me, all that 'stuff' was just boring.

On rare occasions, I would meet an honest and transparent soul and listen patiently as they opened their life up to me. I was young and thirsty for guidance and purpose and hung on every word. In return, I would work hard to find equitable solutions for their financial life.

There was Bill. A brilliant surgeon who, before his retirement, chaired the Division of Neurological Surgery at Vanderbilt Medical Center and was one of the top neurosurgeons in the world. One of the earliest pioneers of frontal lobotomy, he was a revered man with a gentle soul. He trusted me with his life savings, and I honored that with all my heart.

His invitation to me for financial advice might be an unsolicited afternoon call, "Hey, why don't you come over and have a martini and explain this statement I just got in the mail. A brain surgeon could not figure this out. I happen to know this cause I'm a brain surgeon!"

I would drop by after work and talk with him for fifteen minutes about finances and then spend the rest of the night asking him questions about how the mind works. He would lean back, raise his glass, and tell me stories of forty years spent healing others with his hands.

There was Eula. Humble and modest with a quick and engaging intellect, I would share a thousand phone calls and visits with her over the course of a decade. When her mind got feeble, I would finish her sentences for her. It got to the point where I would come to her house and help her go through her mail. She would set up a little card table in her living room, and we would pour over her leather-bound ledgers still using a No. 2 pencil. When she was diagnosed with Alzheimer's, she gave me full discretion of her money. I looked for family and found a nephew who took over for me. When she passed away, most of her two million went to Goodwill, the Salvation Army, and her alma mater, Tennessee Tech — with a room there dedicated to her.

There was John. My first conversation was a cold call at 6:30 pm, which irritated him because I had interrupted his dinner. Eight years later, the family chose me and five others to carry his casket. I could not hang that honor on a wall, but that is what I would rather you know about me than the degrees and certificates you would see behind my desk chair.

There was Dick, the owner of a chain of hardware stores in Alabama. He loved finding negative newspaper articles about my employer. One day I told him I would let him talk to the firm about it. I held the phone up in the air in silence. After five minutes, he hung up.

I called him back immediately and asked him, "What'd they say?" He laughed. Then I gave him the lecture, "I'm only gonna say this once. I do not work for a company. I work for you. Our business is between you and me. Nobody else."

That is how it was back then.

Then there was Helga. I managed a small account for her. She introduced me to her wealthy nephew, Ulrich, who lived in a small town near Düsseldorf, Germany. I fell in love with his family and would go there every year in the fall. They would put me up in one of his many properties, feed me, take me to concerts, parties and show me castles. I would go with them and their friends to homes in Leipzig, cruise the Rhine and drink wine in the Riesling vineyards of Mainz. Ulrich had eight pilots that flew for him. He would take me on his business trips in King Airs to cities in East Germany and Poland. Once, he stopped to help a stranded young mother on the side of the autobahn change a tire. That touched me to the point where I spent the next year learning to speak German, his language, so I could better understand him.

At home, I would regularly fly to small airports. Clients would meet me, give me a car, and invite me to stay in their homes. I held bonds of deep friendship and talked more about thunderstorms than investments. But I felt every bit of the pain of losses and joys of successes that came with the undulating market values of the money they had entrusted me to steward.

My business was good, and in April of 2000, I had my best month ever, grossing over a 100,000 dollars in production. I started getting phone calls and offers from every firm in town. I would decline them, saying I felt too comfortable to leave.

Then one day, I got a ridiculous offer from a larger investment firm, and I accepted it. It was more money than I had ever seen. And it would be the worst business decision in my entire life.

When I arrived at my new office, I saw the mid-six-figure check lying on my desk. My new boss's name was Tony. He was cordial and friendly and introduced me around. I immediately got on the phone and brought almost all my clients with me to our new 'home.' After I got their accounts changed with the new logo, I planned a much-needed vacation.

One of my best friends, Mike, and I decided it would be a good idea to tour Europe on motorcycles. BMW sponsored a High Alpine ride through Bavaria during my favorite time of the year, fall. Plans made, we flew to Munich and were issued bikes. We rode through southern Germany, Austria, Liechtenstein, Switzerland, and Italy over snowy mountain roads with barely a speed limit posted.

We traveled over the Stelvio Pass and the Grossglockner glacier, navigating golf cart-sized paths through remote ski villages. We stayed in 600-year-old hotels and had picnics on mountainsides. For the better part of two weeks, we clocked almost 1,800 kilometers and, at the end, were bone-tired, had beards, and were out of money.

When we boarded the plane for home, we were spent and quickly went to sleep. I woke up hours later, looked out the window, and saw something that startled me. The sun was on our tail.

If you are traveling home from Europe in the afternoon, what you do not want to see is the sun behind you. I had been a pilot for twenty-two years but had never been as frightened as I was at that minute.

I woke up Mike, "Sorry to wake you up, man, but you know we're flying from Munich and landing at 2:00 pm in Philly, right?"

Mike grumbled, "You woke me up to tell me that?" He shifted in his seat, his back to me, fixing to go back to sleep.

Dead serious, I replied, "I woke you up to tell you that it's almost noon, we're heading east, and it's getting dark outside. We ain't going to the States, and we are a long way from Philly. I think somebody's got the plane."

Mike saw the look in my eyes, sat up, rubbed his eyes, and looked outside.

There were a few passengers talking while others slept or read their magazines. The people in front of us raised their heads up over the seat and started asking questions. We were in a packed Boeing 777 with close to 300 passengers on board, many of them now with their heads together in whispers; apparently, I was not the only one that noticed we were not in Kansas anymore.

The plane remained level, and I noticed no steep banking turns. Whoever was flying the plane knew where they were heading, and it was not Philadelphia. We were also losing altitude, the sun quickly dipped under the horizon, and outside our window, the sky became totally dark.

The silence was suddenly interrupted by the speakers above our seats. "Attention, this is the captain. As you probably know by now, we have been rerouted. Please remain in your seats. You are not allowed to move about the cabin. We will be landing in Munich in forty-five minutes."

We had been flying for almost nine hours, and we were landing exactly where we had just departed. Nothing made sense. An older gentleman got out of his seat to check his overhead bin and was promptly tackled and pushed back into his seat by two female flight attendants. A serious hush descended over all of us. We stayed still and waited for the plane to land.

When we finally came to a stop on the tarmac, we were immediately boarded by soldiers with weapons drawn. Gathered outside in a single file line, we were escorted past armored military vehicles and sequestered in a large sealed-off room surrounded by soldiers with machine guns or

MP7s. I spoke to others in my best German, trying to find out if anyone knew what was going on.

There were rumors that New York had been hit by a bomb, the Empire State Building was on fire, and the Pentagon was under attack. As I listened, I quietly removed my American flag fanny pack (don't judge) from around my waist and slipped it into my carry-on bag out of sight — were we in a war?

We were soon loaded into double-decker buses and driven to an unknown location. There were TVs on the bus all tuned into CNN Europe. That is the first we were to see of the Twin Towers collapsing. The scenes were horrific. I could not hear the feed, but the video showing the devastation of the planes crashing into American buildings was being played over and over. I, along with Mike and our fellow travelers, was silent, stiff with shared shock and terror.

It was after midnight in Munich, and we still had no clue where we were being taken. After two hours, we arrived in the small ski town of Schliersee and were organized in lines again and led through the front doors and lobby of a large hotel, where they opened the kitchen and bar for us.

As we entered our respective rooms, we each found the following short note on our pillow:

> US AIRWAYS 015 München–Philadelphia
>
> Dear Passenger,
>
> A Major National Incident has happened in the United States this morning.

> The Federal Aviation Administration of the United States has suspended all air travel to and from the United States until further notice and closed all airports in the U.S.
>
> For this reason, our flight returned to Munich.
>
> We will accommodate you in the Arabella Hotel at Schliersee, which is approx. 2.0 hours from the airport, where you will be served dinner and breakfast tomorrow morning. Tomorrow morning at 8:30 a bus will pick you up from the hotel and bring you back to the airport.
>
> We trust; however, you understand that we are unable to give you any further information regarding your new departure to the United States.

Later that evening, I met Mike in the bar, and we decided to rent a car in the morning and find someplace else to go. A couple of nights later, we were on the small Italian island of Grado on the Adriatic Sea. Being restless, I left Mike to rest and wandered through town. Before long, I was lost. A thunderstorm came up seemingly out of nowhere and knocked out all the power. I found shelter under the dripping awning of a tiny restaurant. I do not think I have ever felt so disconnected. I spent the rest of the late afternoon eating bread and drinking wine with two Italian girls. Being the only customers in the dark candle-lit cafe, we tried our best to have a conversation, albeit a broken one. Even if I could only understand a few words, it was comforting to hear their beautiful singsong language and see their smiles; it felt normal even though it was not.

When we were finally allowed to fly out, five days had passed. On the way back to our connection in Chicago, we flew within a few hundred miles of New York, and out the left side of the cabin's row of windows, we could still see the long column of smoke from the smoldering remnants of the Twin Towers. A thick, dark line against a blue sky that reached vertically to our altitude then sharply angled to the left as it met the Gulf Stream winds. That sight will be forever imprinted in my mind.

Back home, the world had changed. I used to go pick out an airplane, fill out a sheet, come back two days later, and slide a signed blank check under the door of the terminal. Now my small airport was surrounded by razor wire and required a magnetic identity badge to gain access.

At my office building, there were security guards stationed at the door to check my credentials before I was allowed inside. Before long, our firm sold to a Swiss company with a cold and guarded culture. My old friendly manager was replaced with a short, gruff, insecure young bulldog who had the personality of a prison warden with a toothache. He would visit me in my office twice a week and threaten to pull my contract if I did not increase sales. The market was scared. I had my clients protected in defensive portfolios that did not pay much commission, and apparently, that did not sit very well with the bottom line of the new company. By the time my contract was up in 2006, I held my account book in the air like a white flag and sold it to a rookie broker for a four-year share of the commissions. In return, I had to sign a contract forbidding me to contact any of my former clients who had supported me for twenty-one years. At the end of the month, half of us had walked out the door. By 2009 those offices had been dismantled, most of the brokers had scattered, and the markets had lost almost half their value.

The money I received from the sale of my client base lasted three years. Then I had to start borrowing against my home equity to cover child support and private school for my kids. During the Great Recession following the housing market debacle, my income was close to zero, and I quickly racked up over 300,000 dollars in debt. Like so many others on the sinking ship of 2009, I was without a life raft.

In the summer of 2010, I had already calculated how much money I was worth dead and hoped that would get my kids through college. I was at a McDonald's searching for loose change in my truck for lunch when I got a phone call. It was an old friend of a friend, David, the regional manager for a major insurance company, who had heard about my plight and hired me on the spot.

After three months in training with no pay, I had gained the Tennessee territory as a wholesaler for financial advisors. I ranked third out of all hires for that year and sold over 975,000 dollars in commissionable premiums in the first eight months I had been on the road. That gave me a hefty income for a while until that firm was sold, and I was again jobless. I took on a job at a tiny bank that paid little, and in two years, I was hired as a financial advisor at a larger bank which gave me the bump on the resume I used to land the job by which I now held by a thread.

CHAPTER 13
THE STRINGER

IN MY PRESENT predicament, I knew one thing for sure, whomever Linda brings into my office today without an appointment is gonna be well entertained by me; I was probably going to be fired soon. Almost out of options, as slap-happy and dangerous as a thirteen-year-old at a gun range. Even if they did not fire me today, I knew I would not be around soon anyway; my salary cut-off clock was ticking.

Linda knocked on my office door, then quickly ushered in a tall, stately gentleman, "This is Mr. Middleton, and he would like to open an account. I'll just leave you two alone."

She moved behind him, smiled, and winked at me twice. Then pulled the door shut behind her.

I stood up and reached out my hand to shake his, "Mr. Middleton, have a seat."

We both sat down. He sat but did not look at me; instead took out his checkbook.

Without looking up, he barked, "I'd like to open up a custodial checking account. No frills."

"Why would you want to do that?" I asked him.

"Excuse me?" he questioned. At least I got him to look at me.

Keeping it friendly, I replied, "I'm curious. It's a beautiful day outside, and yet you chose to stroll into our bank to open an account. I would just like to know why?"

All business, he replied, "It's a custodial account for my grandson. I'm funding his education."

I lazily answered, "I see. Well, I don't think that's a good idea. Nah. That'll never work."

Blustered, he replied, "Say, what kind of a banker are you anyway?"

His eyes followed mine up the wall just to the right behind my desk to see the New York Stock Exchange membership document signed off to me in 1985, then over to the CRPC certification from 2001, then across to the CFP diploma in 2003, and then the picture of me smiling with Mike Ditka, and finally the master's degree from Prudential Bache in 1999. I looked back at him, scanning all five of my Service Leader of the Year awards from days past.

"Just the best there is," I said, still staring directly into his eyes and smiling.

He rolled his eyes and replied as if to a four-year-old, "Why do you think a custodial account won't fund an education?"

I continued to bring him to the trough slowly, "Because limits on contributions are chicken feed to the ludicrously expensive tuitions that are going up ten percent a year."

Frustrated, he spat out, "I plan on making annual contributions, and he's only three years old!"

I nodded my head and asked, "What's his name?"

Through gritted teeth, he replied, "Dominic."

"Well, Mr. Middleton, I'll probably be dead, but here comes old Dom strollin' in here when he reaches eighteen. The custodial money will all be his, and percentages based on a lot of expensive research say he will just smoke it. It will either go to his ex-wife or Harley Davidson. Yep. Might even go to Jim Beam. Or all three."

He rolled his eyes this time and scratched his head for a minute. Then he quietly asked me, "What would you do?"

I dropped my smirk; I was beginning to like this fella, "529 plan. You keep the money, cook it in the market for fifteen years, then hand it to the college tax-free. If he doesn't go, then keep the money with a ten percent hit. Plus, you could max it out today with a five-year gift straight up if you got the dough." I paused for effect, "Do you have that kind of dough, Mr. Middleton?"

"Oh, I got the dough alright." He sounded defensive.

I sat back in my chair and rolled my eyes, bored. Still smiling.

Then he started to brag, "If I told you I had ten million dollars, what could I do with it?"

I looked him in the eyes and gave him an answer in a short burst, "Title it away from the IRS and the black sheep in the family, parlay a ladder of bonds to satisfy your income need, effectively diversify the rest in a triangle of equity, with options to provide the buffers."

He listened and looked down at his checkbook. Then leaned into me over the desk, "Is that what you would do with the money?"

He wanted an honest answer.

"Me with ten mil?" I thought for a second, "No way, not a chance."

Fed up, he roared, "WHAT?"

I replied, "First, I'd have to see it in cash. Then I'd swim around in it like Scrooge McDuck. Then I'd throw it all in the trunk of my new five-liter Ferrari and drive till I ran outta road, buy an airplane, then an island, and kick back."

Serious now, I leaned toward him, "But that's just me, I'm an ass, but not when it comes to other people's hard-earned money."

He blinked, "Banker, do you have time for lunch."

I smiled, stood, and offered my hand, "That depends, Mr. Middleton. You buyin'?"

FRED MIDDLETON AND I sat at a round glass table in Cafe de Louie in the heart of downtown Nashville, or just "Louie's," as it was called by the locals.

A spunky college-aged waitress took our order.

Fred spoke first, "Give me a burger with fries. Iced tea. And whatever my friend wants."

I ordered boiled shrimp and a martini.

He spoke again to the back of our waitress, "Make that two martinis. Skip the iced tea."

Fred started grilling me, "So how long you been in the money business?"

I answered, "Since '85. Six years after they invented *erasable* ink."

He pressed on, "So, you were a stockbroker then?"

I snorted. Right then, I decided I liked the man; I had really bated him and came out of that meeting without a black eye.

I looked him square in the eye and told him the truth of it, "Back in the day, we weren't so diagnostic. Our financial advice for our clients was that they needed stocks. Unless they already had stocks. In that case, they should sell their stocks and buy our stocks. We were youngsters, "green" they called us. Our manager would go around smoking a big cigar, visit the lot of us in the morning and say, "OK. Here are 10,000 shares of ABCD I just grabbed from underwriting. Now get rid of it." I would cold-call 100 people from the phone book, get hung up on and cussed out from ninety percent of 'em, and sell the stock to the remaining ten. It wasn't very personal, but we hit the allotment if we were lucky and climbed to success on the backs of whomever the shmucks were who bought 'em. If the stock went north, we had another shot at calling 'em back with another hit. If we hit three in a row, it was a hat trick and we had 'em on a stringer. Then we'd trade stocks for more stocks and ride it out till they crashed. That crapshoot, buying and selling, paid two percent in and two percent out. We shared that 40/60 with the firm and then drank toasts at the piano bar around the corner. Early the next morning, we would line up and pitch quarters at the wall, closest kept the pot, until we smelled the cigar smoke, and did it all over again, rinse and repeat. I earned a glass corner perimeter office, a credenza for vodka and vermouth, and an amber ashtray as big as a hubcap. We were the 80s version of *Mad Men*. Yeah. I churned and burned stocks until we all got smoked in the crash of '87. That is when I really started makin' it rich ... with munis."

Fred replied, "Munis?"

I continued, "Municipal bonds, they issue them for every tiny school district and hospital in the country. I'd call folks in small towns and ask them if their school district was any good. Then they would spend ten minutes braggin' about how it was better than Harvard. Then I would tell 'em I had just a few bonds left that were issued to fund a school like Harvard. Those munis would sell like hot cakes. If they bought at least a 100,000 round lot, I'd rent a plane and fly down to visit them."

Incredulous, he asked, "You fly too?"

I nodded my head, "Oh yeah, sure. I got my flying license in '91. I could land at a tiny airport right in their backyard. They would drive to the airport, hug me like a buddy and parade me around town showin' me off to their rich friends. Those friends helped me get new clients, and I ended up selling more bonds for other school districts, hospitals, etc. Got to visit places like Enterprise, Andalusia, Red Level, Tupelo; it was a good gig, fun. And that taught me the most important thing I ever learned about this business."

Fred, "What was that?"

I leaned into him, "I learned where they all kept their real money. The mother lode."

Smiling, Fred asked, "And where is that?"

I took another big sip on my martini, looked him square in the eye, "They kept it next to their heart."

There was a moment of silence, then our waitress came over with our plates of food and sat them down on the table.

Fred took a big bite of his burger. Then said, "You know, I've always been afraid of those puddle jumpers. I had a friend get killed in one of those things."

I put my fork down, "Wow. Bummer. What happened to 'em?"

"He was flying a couple of fishermen into the mountains near Ville-Marie, Quebec, just north of my home. It was a terrible accident, weather-related."

I shook my head, "So sorry. Are you Canadian?"

"An ex-Pat. I'm from Pennsylvania originally. I had a small distributor business in Pittsburgh, chemicals. We sold barrels of sulphuric acid for the tanning industry, soda ash for glass, sulfur for the steel plants. Then I bought into a big company in Toronto twenty years ago and started shipping hopper cars full of the stuff, then barges. Where are you from, banker?" Fred asked, taking another sip.

I smiled, "You're lookin' at it. Born and raised here. Tried to leave Nashville several times, but I guess I always got homesick and came back. Tell you what. Why don't you let me show you around town?"

He nodded, "I'd like to, but I can't. I have a flight out in the morning."

As we talked, the martinis started acting like truth serum. I learned he had family here and was tired of his job. He wanted to be closer to his grandkid and felt guilty of staying away so long from his daughters.

I told him about my divorce and my dad. I told him that I had been retired and wanted to make the most of this opportunity I had been given by the bank. I told him I was looking for a break.

Somewhere in the third martini, the real Fred came out.

He put both hands on his glass, leaned into me, and said in a lower voice, "Look. Somebody offered to stroke me a check. I sold out about two months ago. Thought about living in Tennessee. I come down here to look around and liked it. I found a house in Belle Meade, already started renovations. The plan is to have it finished out in a month. Your bank is doing the closing, and I would like to bring the rest of my nest egg down here."

My stomach did a little flip of happy. Belle Meade was the bluest zip code in the state, Nashville's version of Beverly Hills. We ordered two more martinis.

I took a healthy swig and slurred out, "Congrats! Sounds like we are gonna be best friends then, huh?"

At this point, I believe we were way over the martini limit, apparently causing a stir in the middle of the day with the patrons. I barely focused on the bartender giving our waitress the throat-chop hand signal to his neck.

Fred began slurring, "You sil flyin' dem puddle jumpers?"

I took another swig, "I'm not curr'ntly. If you don't stay flyin' on a constant, they get dan...gerus."

Fred leaned in, "Ya ever had problems up 'ere?"

I laughed through my mid-sip and spat some of my martini at him, hitting his shirt.

Then I sat back, "Yep."

"Tel me a story, banker." He leaned back in his chair too, almost spilling on the floor and catching himself.

I thought for a minute.

"Well. I been lost ... Been in storms ... I floota Savanna Tenissee onct an landid in Korinth Missipee." That started our giggle box.

"Lef my seatbelt outside and opend the door and lost my sellfone over Clarksvll."

We both cracked loud up enough for the people at the next table to move. Our waitress brought our bill to our table. Not happy.

I slurped one more time on my glass, getting louder.

"Hey, Fred ... I wuz on my way fum here ta Biloxi one time ina 172 ... It wuz a warm night ana hadma winda open with my arm hangin out jus daydreemn. It's so peesful up ther ya know ... I like to heer that engine runnin so smoooooth. Then tha next thing I says to maself is HAY! I don't *heer* no engine. Hghhhnnghhhaha!!!" We both were giggling out loud like schoolkids.

He finally regained his composure; his eyes were big. He leaned in close and slobbered to me in a drunken whisper, "So banker, what ... what happnd then?"

I looked up at the restaurant manager, who was now standing beside our table, glaring.

"An thin, I got KIKKED outuv a BAR!!!."

That got us both roaring and then promptly escorted out to the sidewalk.

Fred slapped me on the back and stumbled toward his hotel.

I shouted, "Don miss yer flight!!"

I could hear his laughter as he made his way to the corner, then he turned left and was gone.

I could do nothing more than sit down heavily on a bus bench and lean my head back; I was hammered. Taking in the traffic, the city noises, and finally exhaling, everything faded ...

There was a full moon silvering the edge of wispy clouds in front of me. It lit the swirling mass of mist that bunched and gathered in the valley far below like the smoke that gives these mountains their name. The sky was blue-black too. I had never ventured up the rock this late at night. I took in a breath of crisp, cool, silent air. A gentle roar of wind through the trees caused me to look down, past the moonlit, cracked, red stone that bent and stretched hundreds of feet to the flat earth below. There I noticed two large forms coming out of the tree line. They were bears hunting the hill. One of them looked up and spotted me or caught my scent, most likely. The excellent climber had no problem scaling the folds and was moving quickly in my direction. I frantically searched around my table-sized summit for a place to hide. There was nothing.

I scurried to the other side of the rock only to find another cliff. When I peered over the front edge, the bear caught me in its grasp. I fought his death grip, but he had hold of me and pulled me over with his massive paw. I tumbled as if in slow motion down into the blue mountain mist, hitting my head on the edge.

Thud. "OWWW! NOOOOO!"

I woke up with a start in my bed. I had banged my head on my own headboard. My body was tangled in sheets and blankets. Zeke was peering up over the mess, looking at me like he had seen a ghost.

I reached over to pat his head, "Sorry boy; I thought you might 'a been a bear. Oh Lord, my head."

I held my head in my hands. I was hurting. I looked at the clock; it was four in the morning. I had been 'lights out' for twelve hours. I stumbled to the bathroom and splashed cold water on my face.

I was about to leave a message at the office that I would be taking a sick day and thought better of it. I could not afford to quit now.

I stumbled into the office and ignored the white shirts who were staring at me as I dragged by their offices. When I got to my door, I fumbled with the keys and finally made it to the chair behind my desk.

Linda came in with the coffee, "Late night?"

"Do you have to speak so loud?" I snipped.

"Soorrryyyy." She grinned. "Oh, by the way, Dr. Carnahan just arrived, and he's ready to see you."

Carnahan? I thought. *You mean he did not cancel?*

I quickly logged into my screen with blurry eyes, slurped some coffee down, and tried to get myself composed.

"OK. Send him in." I said with not a lot of confidence.

Linda ushered the good doctor in and shut the door behind him as he took his seat.

I was shuffling papers, trying to look normal.

He waited a minute, watching me very patiently, "How long is this paper business going to take you?"

"Good morning Dr. Carnahan." I sat up in my chair. "About forty-five minutes."

I pulled out a sheet of paper and placed it in front of him, "Here, it's a questionnaire; please go ahead and fill this out, should only take two minutes."

Dr. Carnahan looked at the document, "Why do you need all this information on me? All I want is a recommendation. I need to make more on my money, that is all. What do you recommend I do at this lousy bank anyway?"

He shouted, "I'm the client. Aren't you the expert?"

I held my head, grimacing in pain.

He noticed my discomfort and said, "Are you OK?"

I groaned, "Actually, I feel a little sick. Don't get too close."

Then I leaned too close to him and said thickly, "Can you like, give me a pill?"

He screwed up his face, leaning back as far as he could, "What kind of pill?"

"You know, prescribe me something. Something good. I'd appreciate it."

He looked confused and started out of his chair toward the door.

I pleaded one more time, "Can you at least give me a recommendation? I'm desperate. Please."

He was adamant, "Look. I don't have time for this. I do not know what is wrong with you. Here's my card. Make an appointment. We'll run some tests." He threw the card on my desk.

"Why?" I said, no longer groaning, "I'm the patient. Aren't you the expert?"

He stopped at the door, turned around. I was smiling.

He shook his head, sat down, and listened. We both looked at the clock.

Then I started quizzing him, "Let me ask you something, why did you become a doctor?"

"What's that got to do with my money?" he asked.

"Because I'm trying to make this as quick as possible." I pointed to the clock, "We only have thirty minutes left."

I threw up my hands, "All I know about you is you're a doctor, and you want money, and there's easier ways to make money. I need to know more."

I waited.

"Because my father died with cancer." He blurted out, "And I wanted to fight back."

"Tell me, do you have family now? Any brothers, sisters, kids?" I asked.

"It's just me and my wife," he said, shaking his head.

He explained that when he was a teenager, he had been close to his dad. After his father died, he and his wife had struggled to make ends meet. Medical school had been tough, and they decided not to have kids. Now, at forty-five, he wanted to be able to retire at sixty. He let me know how much he needed to do so. His savings alone was not going to cut it.

I took his age and income and ran through an illustration. He was antsy, checking his watch repeatedly.

"Ever heard of a LIRP?" I asked him.

He checked his watch again, "No."

I began slowly, "At your age and income, you could take advantage of IRS loopholes with life insurance and abuse a cheap IUL, pay premiums for ten years, let it cook in the market for five more, and retire."

I sped up, channeling an auctioneer, "Take the income from principal out tax-free, then borrow income for the rest of your life, also tax-free, and never pay it back. When you die, your wife gets to keep her lifestyle at the club. When she dies, all of it goes to the American Cancer Society and is non-reportable tax-free out the door. It'll work. You will be set for retirement. Doctors do it all the time."

I finished with a flourish, took a breath, and looked at the clock, forty-five minutes exactly. We made it.

"Time's up." I got up and escorted him out. "You will have to make another appointment, have a very nice day."

He nodded, scratching his head like I had just sold him a car he didn't know he needed.

Linda scheduled him for the following Tuesday at 9:00 am sharp.

I practically skipped home that evening; I had two on the stringer. Things were working out.

CHAPTER 14
THE TAMED BEAST

WE CELEBRATE ZEKE'S birthday every December on the 9th. That is the day, according to the shelter, that he was born. How could they know that? He was supposed to be a Catahoula too. His rap sheet from multiple shelters was probably about as accurate as my action plan.

Zeke always gets anxious and restless around his birthday, not because he had the cognitive ability to conceive a year had passed, but because of the lack of hiking and outdoor activity during the cold winter months.

With normal dogs, your walk might be an around the block while conversing on your cellphone with a friend. With Zeke, it might require a map, compass, water bladders, trek poles, and a headlamp. There were few exceptions. I sometimes would start with the ultimatum that it would be a maximum of four blocks. He seemed amenable to that. Then an hour later, I would find myself two miles away, buying bottled water from a gas station I'd never seen before.

I remember the first fresh snow after Alex gave me my gift. I have a picture of Zeke standing sideways on a bridge with the facial expression of a brilliantly painted lawn statue, but which now I recognize as confused delight, body language primed as if he could jump in all directions at once. He was allegedly a one-year-old puppy. My walk with him that day was a Nantucket sleigh ride around the golf course and had resulted in a couple banged up knees, mostly mine, but the memory was worth the bruises watching how he investigated his new white-filled world. I do not know what it is about snow and dogs, but most dogs I've had go crazy with emotions in the white stuff.

That was three years ago. Time had flown by, and he had mellowed into a house pet (with an instruction book for innocent visitors). We still had the 'it's mine if I found it' rule, but even that had tempered to a mostly non-dangerous level. I pulled a birthday cake out of his mouth that year, and I can still type the words on these pages.

He would gaze deeply into my eyes when I gave him praise or a pat. But he rarely offered a direct look otherwise. A fast turn of my head would catch him watching my neckline and cause him to quickly look away. It was as if his uninvited stare might have been considered a challenge.

He still had mongrel habits and would sleep in the warm ashes of an untended fire pit and scavenge food on walks. If I had forgotten a bag of bribes, he would ignore my pleas of "Drop It!" and keep the large rotten carcass he found in his mouth. I was forced to look away and hold my ears as he crunched, then gulped it down, swallowing hair, tail, and all. On one walk in the dark of night, he excused himself with his long leash behind a tree. When he came back to my side, he surprised me with a large opossum he held in his mouth. He wanted to play with his new friend, but when he dropped it, it just lay dead on the road. He finally left it, and later when I looked back, the opossum was gone. One spring day, I stopped and identified a juvenile cottonmouth under the grass by a tree. In two seconds, Zeke had it by its tail and was shaking it like a checkered flag at an Indy race. He dropped it when I screamed bloody murder, and it scurried through the woods to find its mama. Later, on that same trail, he took off after a full-grown deer. The long retractable leash snapped in half as it flew out of my hands. That was the last I saw of them both, until ten minutes later when Zeke limped back, dragging his end of the broken retractable, which was now four feet of frayed cloth, smiling at me and wagging his tail.

Over the last three years together, we had averaged about four miles a day. We knew every field, road, park, and dog-friendly place that existed. We had settled into a routine of sorts. He had his 'milk run' around the neighborhood. We would go to the corner gas station where the girls at the counter would run out and tussle his ears. Then over to Jack's Market where Zeke would sit and wait in line, moving up step for step, as folks finished their transactions until it was our turn. Then he would carefully put his forepaws on the counter and receive a dog bone at eye level. His usual attire was a bright red harness draped with an American flag that accentuated his size and patriotism. Everybody got to know Zeke. He was hard to miss.

CHAPTER 15

THE GATHERING STORMS

ON THE OTHER side of the world, in the Hubei Province of Central China lay the capital city of Wuhan. With a population of over eleven million people, Wuhan is considered the political, financial, cultural, and educational center of Central China. Like other modern sprawling cities in China, Wuhan has an ancient past. It is a cultural collision of shining skyscrapers, airports, and railways, combined with wet markets that sell live fish, poultry, and exotic animals for food consumption. The largest wet market in Central China lies within its city borders on the west bank of the Yangtze River. Before its closure, the Huanan Seafood Wholesale Market boasted a price list that contained not only live poultry, seafood, and livestock but also over 100 wild animal types with over seventy-five different species including birds, reptiles, rodents, and wolf pups.

Inside the market, which spanned an area roughly the size of five football fields, over 1,000 vendors stood at the ready, after a short price negotiation, to slaughter your animals while you watched. Cages were stacked high. Ventilation was poor, garbage and guts piled up on the wet floors.

In January 2020, the Chinese state media reported that a sixty-one-year-old man had been the first to die due to complications from a newly discovered virus. The man had been a regular at the market, along with dozens more who had become sick and were lying in hospitals. Severe Acute Respiratory Syndrome Coronavirus 2, or SARS-CoV-2 for short, was not reported to be humanly contagious, but more research needed to be done. The report of this death came just a few days before the Chinese New Year, when hundreds of millions of people would travel across the country.

Li Wenliang, a thirty-four-year-old physician at the Wuhan City Central Hospital, tried to sound the alarm that a troubling cluster of viral infections he witnessed in the province could grow out of control. He warned colleagues that the virus he observed resembled a SARS virus similar to the one in 2003 that had infected over 3,000 and killed 774. He was arrested, detained under cover of night, and forced to sign a statement denouncing his warning as an unfounded and illegal rumor. He died of COVID-19 less than a month later.

When other cases popped up in Thailand, South Korea, and Japan, the World Health Organization officially declared it a global health concern, and the entire city of Wuhan was shut down, turning into a ghost town overnight. The entire population of eleven million was sequestered at home or in hospital.

When the first case appeared in the United States, a man in his thirties who had just returned from Wuhan, all travel to and from China was quickly banned. By this time over 9,800 people had been infected worldwide. We could only watch the news with trepidation while the more pragmatic rushed to stock up on disinfectant, hand sanitizer, and masks to shield their faces.

The disease which would make its way to every nook and cranny on our planet became known as COVID or the VID.

The symptoms were flu-like or asymptomatic. Deaths usually occurred with underlying health conditions, but not always. It seemed to prey on the immunocompromised and the elderly. It was scary by the eerie way in which it was silently spreading. No one knew if they had it, and testing was so sporadic and clumsy that results sometimes took longer than the disease. A person might be an asymptomatic super-spreader and not even know it. There were even reports it could be spread by dogs.

In the United States, COVID-19 barely made the headlines. Whatever virus stories we heard sounded like somebody else's problem; half the country was convinced it was all a hoax. Our economy remained on solid footing, and the stock markets were trading at all-time highs. We felt that our health experts and resources were the best in the world. All the threats made about previous diseases, SARS, MERS, Bird flu sounded exotic and never made it here. It would more likely appear in a future issue of National Geographic than in the Wall Street Journal. We had plenty other subjects to talk about around the water cooler. We thought.

CHAPTER 16

PROSPEROUS BEGINNINGS

IT FELT GOOD to finally have two promising clients in my pipeline. The whole office noticed the change in me right away. I bounced into work Monday morning, on top of the world, clutching a small bouquet of flowers. I was one of the first at the Keurig and made two cups of fresh coffee, one black and the other sweetened exactly right. I set the sweet coffee and bouquet on Linda's desk, winked at her, and strolled down the hall to my office.

It took her about thirty seconds by my watch to find me.

"Good mor-*niiing*!" I sung.

Linda walked in, sat down, and examined me closely.

"I'm sorry," she uttered politely, "Have we met?"

"Ha-ha." I quipped back. "You're lookin' at the new me."

Not buying it, she asked, "What happened? Did a tree branch fall on your head during one of those death excursions into the woods you go on?"

I laughed, "No. And they are called hikes."

Suspicious, she asked, "So why the change then? You know I'll find out, plus, there happens to be a killer virus out there, why all the happy-go-luckiness? You can't keep secrets from me ..."

I smiled, "Listen, how would you like a raise?"

That got her attention fast. "Excuse me, I have to go," she said. "I am going to find the broker I'm working for and tell him there's a kook in his office."

I waved her to sit down, "Stop, I'll level. You get two percent of my commissions, right?"

She nodded her head. "Yeah."

"Well, Mr. Fred Middleton just sold his stake in his company. Linda, he is moving here, just bought a small mansion in the Meade and our mortgage guys are doing the closing. That will happen in about a month. In the meantime, he's bringing us the check."

Her eyes widened, "How much?"

I silently counted out on my fingers, "Somewhere in the eight figures, maybe?"

She sat forward, "Holy moly!"

I went on, "And that's not all. Dr. Carnahan and his wife are probably going to bite on a LIRP."

Her eyebrows raised, "A LIRP?"

"A LIRP is a big insurance policy, a Life Insurance Retirement Plan. They are thinking about a 200,000 premium ten-pay. Which means that we can wad up our action plan and throw it in the rhubarb. That means you and I can plan a trip. Where you wanna go?"

She gave me a side-eye with a smirk.

"OK. Maui it is. But I was hoping you would say Europe," I said with disappointment.

"I just got two questions for you," she said, all business now. "What color were the mushrooms you found in the woods, and how many did you eat?"

I finished my coffee, "Don't believe me then. Just buzz me if either Middleton or Carnahan calls. In fact, use the loudspeaker."

She got up, threw me one last smirk, and slipped out the door. I think I saw a twinkle in her eye.

When I got home that evening, Zeke noticed the change too. I quickly doffed the suit and donned the cargo shorts, grabbed Zeke's leash and harness, then out the door we ran. Halfway around the greenway through the golf course and an hour later, we were both in the creek. I was skipping rocks over his head, and he was yelling with his squirrel voice. We waded over to the deepest part of the creek and swam under a trestle just as a train was approaching. I pulled on Zeke's leash and ran up the bank toward the roaring train, shouting, "THIS WAY, BOY!"

We quickly scrambled up the steep rocks to the tracks, stopping just feet from the rushing train. The barreling wind from the freight cars blew my cap clear off.

I was the first to start barking, "BAROOOOHHH, BAROOOOOHHH!"

Zeke followed my lead, "BUUURRROOOOOOO!!!" Head back, eyes closed, barking for all the world to hear.

CHAPTER 17
THE WINDS OF MISFORTUNE

IT WAS A beautiful spring day in early March, unseasonably warm for Tennessee. Zeke and I were not complaining. We walked over to the golf course, sat on the fairway, and watched the sunset. It had been a while since I had felt rich. I was looking forward to the next day and the day after that.

I thought back about how hard at times the struggle had been. I had been a single dad since my boys were babies. The balance between work and family was tough. I took off every Wednesday, and every weekend the first ten years of their lives in the hopes I would be able to be with them. I spent years chasing their taillights just to see them grow. Sometimes it happened, and sometimes it did not. I know what it is like to sit at a Mapco gas station in Louisville, Kentucky, eating a corn dog at midnight after driving 200 miles, just to see if I would be invited to a Thanksgiving meal with the boys the following morning. Waking up in the front seat in a rumpled suit with a bad case of heartburn more than once.

I gave up dating women when the kids were young because it would not have been fair; it was all work and all boys, and not enough space in between.

My youngest, Anthony, now twenty-six, had just married Elsa, a sweet, intelligent girl from the Netherlands, whose doe-colored eyes are framed by soft brown hair and razor-sharp bangs, who speaks five languages and has quickly learned to speak Zeke. I could not have done better if I had picked her out of a Neiman Marcus Christmas catalog.

Alex, at twenty-seven, is dating a charming Alabama girl already talking rings; it looks like my little family is growing. I was now a true empty nester, well, except for a 100-pound blanket stealer.

The sun went down slowly, and Zeke and I watched as it slipped under a bank of cumulonimbus clouds that were building in the west with their anvil shapes, each with the flickering luminescence of lightning. Just an overgrown boy in cargo shorts and his dog on a deserted golf course, our backs to the east, watching as twilight formed an infinite sky filled with stars. It had been a good start for the week; I felt more hopeful that evening than I had in a long time. By the time we got home, we were asleep the minute we hit the sack.

I was startled awake by a loud bomb of rolling thunder mixed with the sounds of tornado sirens. The strobe lightning mixed with the wild, whipping, wind noises outside roused me out of bed quickly. Checking my clock, it was just after midnight. Every local television station was updating the progress of five active tornadoes that were violently trekking across Tennessee and Kentucky, the closest of which was an EF3 just two miles north of my bungalow, heading toward Alex's neighborhood.

Zeke and I ran out in the backyard to witness it as it roared from west to east. I checked his countenance to see if the crazy wind and sirens had shaken that poker face, but he just stood beside me, matter-of-factly.

I called Alex first because he was now in the direct path, he answered immediately. He and several others were sheltering in the middle of his complex, blind to the storm's proximity. I kept him on the phone until it passed his location and continued its easterly course. It had just decimated my local airport, reducing every building to rubble and mangling every airplane I had ever flown. Later, rolling through downtown Nashville, the downpour of rain that had accompanied the tornado had flooded my office and rendered it unusable.

The storm would continue swallowing up real estate until it earned the right to be the

sixth-costliest tornado outbreak in this country's history, killing twenty-five people and racking up over one and a half-billion dollars in damages.

The next day I was out early to see the damage and to see my son. I just wanted to give him a hug. His neighborhood was a mess, many restaurants and stores were flattened with bricks scattered everywhere, and fallen trees littered impassable roads.

I called Linda, who let me know our offices would not be opened for a few days as cleanup would take a while. I would have to cancel the meeting with Dr. Carnahan. He is a busy man and difficult to schedule. I knew it would take at least two weeks to get him back in the office. He was getting a little nervous as the Dow had dropped fifteen percent due to the pandemic panic in the latter part of February, but it was rebounding nicely, and I was hoping to get him in soon before the market recovered.

In my business, timing was everything, and the tornado had caused a setback in my planning. I lucked out and was able to schedule him for mid-March at another bank branch location. I made sure he was comfortable about signing the deal. But I prayed the markets and weather would cooperate long enough to get his signature.

The next call was to Fred Middleton, who was almost ready to close on his property and transfer the funds. We just needed the contractors to finish the buildout on his house, and so we could close on that same property to make the transfer legal and my future secure.

NEWS BEGAN TO trickle in about the coronavirus in China, which had now officially become a pandemic. There had been no cases reported in Tennessee, but that was to change on March 8th when a man who had traveled from Boston to Memphis had been diagnosed with the strange and deadly disease. There was a second in Nashville, and on March 12th, the governor declared a state of emergency. The SEC canceled its Basketball Tournament for the first time in its history, dating back to 1933. The NBA and the NHL announced a suspension of their seasons after Utah Jazz forward Rudy Gobert tested positive for coronavirus. By March 13th, the Tennessee legislature ceased its proceedings and vacated the courthouse, and the Grand Old Opry closed its doors. The music was silenced on Broadway, and Nashville was officially in quarantine.

On March 15th, our firm initiated an evacuation on all but the most essential workers. The rest of us were sequestered at our homes, connected only by a VPN broadband network that was spotty at best. I had to cancel my appointment with Carnahan again, and the markets resumed their brutal downward spiral.

The U.S. declared a national emergency, and the Center for Disease Control and Prevention (CDC) recommended no gatherings of fifty people or more. In a week, that number would be reduced to ten. The European Union barred any outside travelers beyond its bloc, and the Tokyo Olympics were canceled. By the end of March, most major countries had initiated hard lockdowns. The U.S. led the world with over 87,000 cases and over 1,000 deaths; the end was nowhere in sight.

The stock market had responded by dropping over 11,000 points (the biggest point drop in its history) and had fallen over thirty-eight percent from its high. The country was heading into another recession. I tried to call Carnahan again but had no luck. The firm had little sympathy for its advisors as they had been sent home with their computers and were still connected to the bank's network. That is all well and good if you have a fat book of clients that needed consoling, but try prospecting in an environment like that with people you just cold-called and see how many are willing to invest their life savings with you on Skype. Not a one. My excuses were beginning to wear thin on management who looked to me for revenue. Carnahan was not answering; I was losing him.

Linda called early one morning at the beginning of May. It was good to hear from her.

"So how are things, I mean outside of Armageddon?" I quipped.

Hesitantly she answered, "Well not too bad since they have the VPN thing straightened out. Getting docs back from clients has kind of been a nightmare, but so far, so good. How are things with you?"

Always optimistic, I answered with a too-loud voice, "Great. The dog and I have been sequestered so long together we're finishing each other's sentences."

She did not laugh, "Well, I have some bad news for you."

I knew that tone in her voice. "Aw Linda, don't tell me you wanna cancel that trip to Maui ... but that's OK; I think I'd rather go to Antarctica to wait this one out anyway."

She interrupted me, "I heard from Dr. Carnahan."

I was listening.

Quickly she blurted out, "He called me an hour ago to say that he changed his mind and hoped you'd understand."

That hit a nerve. "He couldn't call me himself to tell me that?"

She pressed on, "He said he and his wife had discussed it. The call was brief. I told him I would have you reach out to them, but he told me that he had placed his accounts on the 'Do Not Call' list, and so now for you to do so would violate the firm's policy."

I was silently stewing, thinking about what I would tell management. He was one of two of my most promising opportunities, and they knew it.

Linda broke the silence, "I'm so sorry."

Just then, I realized I still had one more chance. “Linda, get Middleton on the phone. Try to reach him any way you can.”

I needed to open Fred Middleton’s account and transfer the funds over from his Canadian bank. My mind was racing.

“How are we going to open a Canadian account?” Linda asked. “That’s against the treaty. The firm won’t allow ...”

I stopped her in mid-sentence, “Just fill out the paperwork with his U.S. address. He will be closing on that house and actually living there soon anyway. If we can get his wet signature in a FedEx down here, we can transfer the funds right away. Understand?”

I had Fred on the phone within the hour.

“Hey, banker! How’s things there in the states? They suck here.”

I tried to sound positive, “Say, we were just talking about you. How about we go ahead and open the brokerage account through this mess so we can get the cobwebs cleared for your transfer. Just the paperwork.”

“Well, they haven’t finished with the house yet. I thought we had to officially close on the mortgage first. I’m not done with the reno; they messed up the patio and got the fireplace on the wrong side. Idiots.”

I lied, “Yeah, we don’t have to wait for that.”

Pretty sure my desperation was showing, but I continued, “We can send you your account docs overnight, and you can forward it back to us with your John Doe. Piece of cake.”

He hesitated but then, “OK, sure that’ll work.”

My relief was palpable, “I’ll have the package out to you today. It’ll be there two days at the latest.”

Linda got the package out that afternoon. And I told myself what I had done was a smallish white lie for the greater good; things would work out before any federal agents were the wiser. Life was good again.

CHAPTER 18
THE LEASH TIGHTENS

I HAD NO time for Zeke and no time for walks. I only had about two more weeks to put this thing together to save my career.

The package arrived from Canada as promised, and we quickly opened the account. It just had to be cleared through compliance.

My phone rang. It was Middleton, "Hey banker, you get the papers?"

I answered, "Yeah, they came yesterday. We got your account open. It should be cleared for the transfer any day."

Middleton was upbeat, "That's good because I can't fly down. The airlines put a stop on U.S. travel from here. The idiots still haven't finished the buildout, and we can't close until they do. Everything is stalled until this craziness is over. At least my funds will be in good hands!"

The last thing he said had me worried. This *craziness* may not be over until a vaccine has been found. That could take a year.

"Tell you what," I told him, "as soon as hear we from the bank we'll transfer the funds and worry about the rest later. Sound good?"

He agreed, "Yeah, that'd be great to get this over with, Eh?"

I love Canadians.

All I had to do to save my neck was get that ten million here safe and sound in his account. That would get management off my back, and I could live nicely off the revenue stream it would produce.

I checked the account every day. I checked the balance. I checked the status of the documents. I checked with the mortgage guys to see if they had closed on the house. We waited for days with no word from Account Transfers.

Then the worst happened. I logged in one day and saw one word next to the account, "Frozen."

I got Linda on the phone pronto, "You see the Middleton account? What is going on? It's frozen; that is a hell of a problem."

Linda comforted me, "It's probably a mix-up because the bank still has his Canadian address. I'll call them right now and straighten it out."

I knew Linda could fix anything. This was her area. She had the contacts and experience.

I paced for two hours, waiting for her call. *Patience*.

The phone rang. Finally.

It was Linda, "Hey. I found out what's wrong."

I quickly snipped, "All I want to know is, is it fixed?"

She answered, "No."

Still snippy, I asked her, "And why not?"

She paused and then spoke, "Because I'm afraid this is a big, big major problem."

There was that tone in her voice that I remembered I don't like. She proceeded to tell me why my world would disappear from below my feet. Why my career was going to vaporize. Why I was such a loser.

She explained that compliance had tried to mail some correspondence to Fred at the U. S. Address we had used to open the account, the very same addresses where according to Fred, there were multiple idiots on hand redoing an outdoor fireplace, but apparently unable to accept a

FedEx. The package had been returned to the bank as undeliverable.

She went on painfully, "When compliance checked with our mortgage department, they found out that the property was vacant and under construction."

They deemed that we were attempting to open a brokerage account for a Canadian citizen with no domicile in the U.S., which is illegal. The account had been frozen pending an investigation.

I was silent as a trickle of fear crawled up my spine.

Investigation? How could it have come to this? It had all seemed so innocent.

I was toast. I had lied to compliance about a foreign citizen. The fact they would open an investigation was ridiculous, but I now had the full attention of compliance, the address was under scrutiny, the client was not closing, and there would be no account, and I was in no place to bargain with my meager offering of a promise of prospect. My action plan had run dry, and I had a meeting scheduled with my manager Frank in three days.

I went flush. What had I done?

"Hey Linda ... I'll talk to you later, I gotta think ... Oh, and thank you. Thank you for everything you have done for me. And I really mean that." I hung up the phone, not waiting for her reply.

There was nothing to do but give in to the fact that I was done. I looked around for clutch holds; I searched my mind for possibilities to bring in revenue to keep me from being spit out of such a predicament and found none. The pandemic, the tornadoes, the crashing markets, and my stinking bad judgment had all collided into a perfect storm to finally finish me off. My dream of a nice fat retirement faded.

Linda tried to call me back, but I didn't answer. Instead, I wrote her a text letting her know that I would be taking my vacation days. Then I threw my phone in the kitchen trash bin and stared at the wall.

Sometime later, I looked in the kids' old rooms. They were empty except for the bookcase. I looked at it more closely. There was a picture of me on an old racing bike I used to own. A YZF-R1, reflective TF blue. I remember that bike; I remember laying down on it at 150 in fifth gear. It's funny about being on a motorcycle at that speed; the two hollow aluminum wheels spinning beneath you become affixed gyros. If you have ever played with gyros on a string, you have witnessed their resistance and stability. It's hard to change lanes on a bike going that fast without throwing a knee out and tugging it over with your weight. I would need to do that if I saw something in the road. My sights were locked on a distant imaginary half-mile dot on the four lanes of clear interstate ahead of me; nothing else mattered.

It was 6:15 in the morning on a Saturday in the spring of 2002. I had just heard that my ex was getting remarried that weekend and moving out of state. I was terrified of the growing landscape between my boys. I was desperate with the thought of losing the two little lives that made mine worth living. I could not shake the feeling that I was fighting an uphill battle, that I had just become the creepy dad that slept in his car hoping for an invite, that perhaps they would all be better off without me.

It was a clear dry road, and my *bright blue lightbulb on wheels* wanted more. I started to shift into sixth gear to reach 200 ...

No. All I could see was my boys.

I came to my senses and released the throttle. The bike displayed a wobbly complaint and belched out a low sad groan of disappointment. I raised a full helmet length above the tiny, cupped windshield and sobered my thoughts.

I rode through the places where I would visit once every Wednesday and every weekend to see my sons. I searched through the old neighborhoods. The familiar streets brought back memories of hopeful thoughts about the adult men they would one day become. How could they grow up to be successful and happy with their own families if I put my needs before theirs?

Sitting erect on the bike, I crept to a stop in front of the house. For ten minutes, I thought of my two young boys in that front yard, growing up in moments. I told myself life was not fair but that they would be OK. That I could never abandon them even if I wanted to abandon myself. Then I started the bike up and drove slowly back to my empty home.

I jerked back to the present. Remembering that I have been to that place before when I thought I was done. Was this now what would finally break me, had I run out of roads?

It was a Friday, late morning. My heart rate was well over 100 beats a minute. I was sitting on the boy's old bedroom floor sobbing my eyes out.

Zeke must have heard me and came slowly loping up the stairs. That was only the second time he had seen me cry. The first time had been years ago when I had fixed his fence in the backyard the very same night he ruined my big future plans, the night he was foisted on me. He tilted his head at me and stared. He was trying to read my mind again, like the many times when he thought I was giving him up at the park. What did this accident-prone, hand biting, poker-faced, food hoarding, squirrel crazy, mongrel escape artist want from me?

I yelled, "Go away! Don't you know I am no good? Go, go lay down and chew something else I can't replace. Damn it, Zeke, go, get out!" I put my head in my hands and moaned between gulping sobs.

When I finally looked up, Zeke had not budged. Instead, keeping my gaze, he got low on his haunches and inched up to my side like a creeping cartoon burglar.

I leaned into him, dug my head in the ruff of his neck, and begged his forgiveness.

"I'm sorry, boy, you didn't deserve that. You're a good dog."

Zeke then laid down, put his head on my lap, and exhaled. If I had not been so sunk in my own sorry state, I would have realized then that that one simple gesture was a first.

I spent that day and the next on my couch, only getting up to let Zeke out to pee, and even then, he did not want to leave my side, glancing up as he went out the back door with a "Are you sure you're OK?" look.

I do not remember putting on his leash. I do not even remember leaving the house. I just remember walking. I did not know our destination. I did not care. I was following Zeke as he led me down a main street that headed downtown, his normal sled dog speed dialed down to a human pace. A thousand thoughts raced through my mind. The game was up. I had lost.

The empty street ahead was devoid of cars. The sidewalk was clear and straight and long and stretched to a point in the far distance. I could see the tops of the skyscrapers ahead of us. Everything was eerily quiet. We were the only witnesses to the traffic lights that changed for no traffic.

The sun felt good on my face. The silence was exactly what I needed. Zeke steadily led me through a wilderness of telephone poles, curbs, parking meters and streetlights, instead of trees and waterfalls.

When we arrived in the epicenter of downtown, there was no music there to greet us. On any normal day of the year, Broadway was stacked side by side with bars that floated Country, Jazz, and Rock'n'roll from their doors at passersby. Now they were silent. The life-sized signs of cowboys strumming guitars and the still-lit neon lights seemed garish, spooky.

No buses, no Ubers, no people, no farm tractors, no foot-pedal bars, no locals, no tourists. We entered with no invitation and received no welcome or admonishment. We stopped at a skyscraper with blue-tinted windows and stood as sole reflections along its base; tall, looming structures filled the area behind us. It was sometime early afternoon. I was not sure. I had no watch, no phone.

The city was barren, forfeited, conquered by a tiny unseen, unknown microscopic virus that had decided to drift through the air and cleanse a city of two million. Life had come to a halt for me and for everybody else regardless of wealth or disparity, money, or title. This sobering thought was what jolted me out of my funk. I was going to record this once in a millennium event forever.

CHAPTER 19
THE TOP OF THE WORLD

IN THE BATTLE that raged between mankind and virus, the humans were losing badly. There were now over a million new cases of COVID-19 added every week. Despite lockdowns in virtually every city across the globe, people were getting sick, and many hospitals were overcapacity. In New York City, bodies were being stacked in refrigerated semi-trailers waiting to be buried. Microscopic invaders infected every soul they could. The effect the resulting disease had on economies was staggering. Some industries like restaurants, hospitals, airlines, and those that involved travel or tourism were laid to waste, while those that involved digital communication, groceries, drugs, alcohol, and streaming TV had thrived and grown more prosperous.

The biggest complaint I heard from the lips of the humans were those of the pains of isolation and the feeling of being 'socially distanced.' In the weeks that followed my downfall, being 'socially distanced' did not cross my mind as a bad thing. Zeke and I were quite comfortable alone. And I became quite comfortable avoiding the compliance folks.

Zeke walked me daily. The phone I carried with me was my

compass, map, flashlight, and weather status. Rarely was it ever used for communication or clock, and most definitely not to answer Frank's calls.

We had abandoned time zones and purpose, and occasionally our trek would involve only the nocturnal where we would slink invisibly through the dark old alleyways in the neighborhood of my bungalow, examining the moonlit backsides of weathered garages and old horse stables, shaped by years of human habitation.

Often, Zeke and I would start a domino effect of barking dogs, each protecting their own 50 x 150-foot square, one by one announcing to the next our route until we would turn right or left, leaving their discourse behind. We were always silent. We had the minutes and hours to study this strange new world. Mankind, almost overnight, had become connected by a common denominator that was taking over the world, and all were laid helpless in its wake.

My problems were not amplified by this condition but rather made bantam in comparison. In fact, my current predicament afforded me the luxury of time to ponder everything but my own stupidity.

Daily, I was fascinated by the display of our human behavior, how we are all biologically the same, and yet so different that, even when faced with a common global terror, we were not capable as an intellectual species to agree on a social solution. If the whole world of humans had shut down for five weeks, the virus would have been starved out of existence, and the threat would have been eliminated. And I would still be facing a firing squad on Monday.

My immediate problems had dissolved in this melee of suffering and death tolls. It was like the confusion of post-9/11 when I preferred getting lost on an island instead of sleeping at the airport; my mind could not conceive the breadth of loss and pain, much less the solutions needed to get past it all. I had reached a point in my life where I stopped trying to fix the future. My mind was planted firmly, episodically in the moment. I was on a dog's leash. Tonight may have us rousting out a gaze of raccoons from a sewer drain and tomorrow laid out under a bright sun in a sea of yellow winter cress.

During the last few days of my hastily taken 'vacation,' Nashville closed its parks because of COVID, and Zeke and I took advantage of it. Now leashless and undetected, we roamed for miles off-trail into places where I had been but never really seen. We would sneak into parks while leaving the car parked on deserted roads. I still followed Zeke; he was the responsible pack leader now. We read no signs and often entered public lands by crossing through creek beds and fence rows instead of trailheads. I would laugh out loud at his way of travel, like a soldier running ahead drawing fire in a zig-zag blur.

We would start out on the edge of some back-country woodland; then I would try to match his reconnoitering in vain, finally watching his receding silhouette mingle and dissolve into the complicated landscape.

On our last day before I would be brought up on charges of fraud, I decided to try a park I had not yet taken Zeke to, Belle's Bend, which lay on the outskirts of the city. An even mix of woodland and grassland with wide trails through groves of maples, oak, walnut, and flowering trees: redbud, Bradford pear, dogwood, among many others, this day it was especially beautiful. These public lands had gained a reprieve from the sequestered humans and were flourishing minus the methane, noise pollution, and McDonald's wrappers. The sky was bluer, the trees greener, the air cleaner, the wildlife bolder. Its recent beauty bore the positive side effects of the absence of human interference. Music to my ears.

Following Zeke, I half ran the perimeter of the 800-acre Belle's Bend of the river, from which the park got its name, trying to keep up with him. I had walked this area plenty when I was a kid, but today the grass was like a carpet beneath our feet.

We spotted a grazing herd of deer a quarter mile away in a meadow of sage grass. Zeke burst into top speed and, within a half-minute, was on their heels. The reaction of the deer was to scatter, to which Zeke first hesitated, then turned and soon was lost among them as they vanished through the forest in the distance.

I continued to walk in the direction of a bank of trees ahead, toward the mighty Cumberland River that bent, flowed, and framed the city of Nashville. Almost 700 miles long and 600 feet wide, the Cumberland is the second largest river in Tennessee. Most likely named for the Duke of Cumberland in 1758, prior to that, it was called Wasioto by the Shawnee Native Americans, who lived here before the settlers. It sat like a giant horseshoe, its tips starting in West Kentucky and ending in East Kentucky with the curve dipping clear across upper Tennessee. Its falls, basins, and forks enveloped by many state parks provided for magnificent hiking, fishing, and outdoor play, to name a few.

Today, the river was angry. Given the number of storms that had swept through recently, the water was rolling fast; I could see whirlpools and small white-capped waves, large timber popping up and then quickly disappearing in the dark rolling swells, a hindrance to the barge traffic that navigated against the current, and dangerous to recreational boaters and swimmers. But that did not matter today because we were in a pandemic and everyone was safe at home watching Netflix, or their eyes glued to the constant barrage of bad news on CNN.

I was tired. My legs cramped. I was getting old. When I had been a younger man traversing these woods, my feet had been guided by future goals, my mind by dreams of lofty ambitions. Now I found myself meandering with no destination in mind, a disastrous future, my ambition tainted by greed. For much of our walk, I had not cared where I was or where Zeke was off to, we were just going, and I had been good with it, but my body ached and needed rest. I heard Zeke thrashing through the trees not far off and called out to him as I neared the river's edge.

It was a warm afternoon and getting warmer fast. I sat down on a grassy rise above the thrust and pitch of the Cumberland. Looking down, it occurred to me that getting to the water today would be tricky; the thicket of river birch, oak, sycamore and sweetgum trees, whose branches were tightly joined along with the weeping willows, were bent over the fast-moving river's edge like a line of can-can dancers taking a bow. The waterline was now up above the tree roots. Without a shore due to the high water, the bushy young sweetgum and ash made it near to impossible to traverse through the busy tangle to reach the river. I closed my eyes and saw Granddaddy Edgar's face the morning I was leaving for college; how proud he had been to confide in me that he had never once in all his life earned a rotten dollar. What would he think of me now?

I brushed the wet from the sides of my eyes. I let my breathing become steady, my mind free from the habitual stress I had grown accustomed to, and in short order, my world went silent, limp.

The deep blue sky above me was adorned with a silvery layer of cotton cumulus. My mixture now consisted only of sky, earth, the invisible wind that brushed my cheeks, and my thoughts. My senses were sharp, focused only on the singularity of this moment, save for the pleasantness I wanted to increase within me. The sound of the gurgling waves of water blended with the wind. The ground melded with the curves on my back, my head on the soft grass. My breathing became steady. My world went numb, dead, silent. The swirling river current surrounded my brain and covered it; all the vibrations of life ceased. There was a void of sensation. Nothing.

I HEARD FAINT bells; then they were again getting louder; I recognized them; they were cowbells. I knew those cowbells. "It's Charlie!" I heard all the kids say almost at once. The sound of gears whined, and around the corner came the old farm Cub tractor, with a square of plywood for a seat covered in circus red and white checkered thick vinyl under a homemade awning adorned with the large clanging bells. Charlie, our beloved ice-cream man, stopped his homemade apparatus in the middle of my neighborhood and was immediately surrounded by a pack of excited kids, hands out with quarters in the air, while he reached into a cooler of dry ice and distributed as many popsicles as quickly as he could to the sea of grubby little waving hands.

I reached in my pocket but did not have a quarter. I turned behind me; in the corner of our yard, there was my dad painting the finishing touches on two bicycle frames that hung on a clothesline. Mine was the candy apple red one with the metal-flake sparkle. My dad looked up at me right then, gesturing his accomplishment in a comical bow. I laughed and stuck my hands in my pockets as the cowbells receded into the distance.

In the alley behind our house, I put the kickstand down on the pull-start minibike I had struggled to get in the side of a VW bus that was packed to the gills. It was no use. I argued my position to my girlfriend in the passenger seat, but she had little sympathy as she told me the only responsible thing to do was leave the bike and quit the band. It was time to grow up, and unless I wanted to live without her this last year of college, I needed to decide fast. I sat down in the driver's seat and looked over at her pretty pout, and made up my mind to quit the band.

I aired my grievance over my decision in the headset to the old man with the white hair who sat behind me in the Piper J-3. We were flying blind in the bowels of a raging storm. He listened to me but was mute as he strained and fought with the control stick between his knees. The plane pitched, yawed, and rolled in severe angles as he attempted to negotiate the turbulence. It was no use. The small plane stalled and fell out of the sky, crashing into a wooded hill.

I staggered out of the plane into a fog. Beyond the fog, there was the plume of a waterfall, which I passed through to the ridged wall of slate before me in the clearing. The moon illuminated the panels of smooth stone, and beyond that, ghostly pairs of glowing red eyes followed me in the darkness. They watched me intently as I crept to the top of the mountain in the starry night but did not advance me this time. I pressed my foot on the first square edge of the rock, then my other foot found another higher step, and I continued to ascend the rock. My foot slipped on the wet ledge as I climbed, and crumbled stone fell and disappeared into the black void beneath me. I closed my eyes tightly and searched another sharp edge above my head which cut into my fingers as I pulled myself up the vertical face of the mountain. I could see the cliff above me; its safety beckoned. One last push up, and I found the corner of the crest of stone, pulled my body over it with great effort gaining solid earth beneath my knees. I fell hard on its cool, flat, horizontal surface. I had made it to the top of the world, bleeding and tired but alive.

Looking at the flat world below, I studied the painstaking trek I had made. I now stood steadfast, determined to stay here and not return to the mess below. I looked to my right, and there was Zeke by my side, soaking wet.

He opened his mouth and spoke, but his words were incomprehensible.

The sun had moved, the shade now on the other side of the oak; my forehead was on fire. He threw back his head and let out an ear-piercing howl. This was like nothing I had ever heard before; not even the coyotes had elicited this earth-shattering shriek.

The muscles in my face twitched as I tried to scream over his howling. I became aware of my heaviness on the grass and awoke to reality; I guessed that I had been asleep for over an hour. I quickly raised into a sitting position and called out to Zeke.

I could hear him splashing and yelping far below me. This was not his squirrel bark; this was a wailing cry for help. He had to be in the throes of the river. Although he had become a pretty good swimmer, I knew he was in trouble.

I rolled over to gain my footing and scrambled my way over the large rocks following the sound of his watery yelps but was blocked by the wall of trees.

I threw myself on the ground to get a look through a gap in the brush; I could see his snout and his long boney forelegs bicycling the air.

He had been carried downstream a hundred feet from my spot, and the mighty current now held him wedged and pinned between the low hanging trees near the bank. He was struggling, snapping out wet barks with his head half underwater.

I called for him, “Zeke! I’m coming, buddy; hang on!”

I slung myself inside the gap and crawled through the woody labyrinth of trees toward him. I fought every branch and bramble that poked, scraped, and tried to slow my progress. Had I misjudged this route? Should I have tried to go upriver and find a bank? I stopped thrashing and listened, worried I was going in the wrong direction.

His screams went silent, and for minutes all I could hear was my heart pounding in my chest. My shirt caught in a tree branch which stopped me in my tracks. I struggled to break free and shot out of the gap falling to my knees, tripping, and rolling into the river. I grabbed onto the first rock as I hit the swift current, propelled downstream at breakneck speed. Holding my head above water, there was nothing left to do but let go of the rock and let the river draw me to where I had last seen Zeke.

As I was carried along, I looked behind me and saw a large log coming up behind me as if we were in a race with each other. I ducked underwater just as it came up on me. I felt it graze the top of my head, but the water was so cold I ignored the hard scrape it gave me and sank under it. I came up gasping for air and threw my hands out to grab onto anything solid. I needed to slow my speed, so I did not pass him but had to keep my feet curled up underneath me so I would not catch on any rocks; the force of the water would pull me under for good. I swam with every bit of strength I had, flailing at the bank when my hand hit a soft rock. I knew immediately it was him. Using one free hand, I grabbed ahold of a fistful of seal-like skin in a death grip, and with the help of thousands of gallons of river torque pushing me from behind, I managed to pull him from his trap between the rocks. He was alive; I could feel him struggle against me.

I flipped over on my back and held his head above water as I scanned the bank for any large rocks that I may be able to use to stop us long enough to make it out. I could feel the heat of the sun, his shivering body, and a rush of warm liquid running into my eyes, but I only had one free hand to navigate with as I struggled to keep our heads above water.

I swam one-handed with all my might and soon hit the bank under a tree whose roots I was able to grab.

In seconds Zeke twisted out of my grasp and bounded over me, scrambling and slipping, up through the maze of greenery.

I pulled myself up, waded out of the water, and stumbled through the strand of densely packed trees until I was let out into the clearing.

In front of me stood a trembling half dog, half bear. I fell upon him and smothered him with hugs. “You damned dog!” I scolded him, “Are you trying to kill the both of us?”

I laid beside him, holding onto him until he rose and shook his huge body from bow to stern, dousing me with a spray of cool water.

Zeke circled me, then looked back at the river with a snort of satisfaction; he was happier than I had ever seen him. He had been outrun by deer and half-drowned by the river and had been thrilled by it. By God, this dog was something else.

I had to catch my breath. I focused on the sounds of the river, pondering its powerful forward movement. It was like time itself, unstoppable. I thought about the fevered dream I had had; it was so vivid, and its message so clear to me. I knew what I needed to do.

I wiped the sweat from my face and noticed my hand was covered in blood. I felt the top of my head; it was sticky with it.

We walked slowly back to the car, but not before we sat down on a dirt knoll and watched the sun go down on a tree line behind a large meadow of wildflowers. The purple twilight finally darkened the field where fireflies, by the thousands, glittered in the mist.

CHAPTER 20

LETTING GO THE LEASH

THE NEXT MORNING, I got up early, shaved, and showered for maybe the first time in two weeks.

I looked like hell. I had proof of the sense that had been knocked into me last night. The top of my head was bruised and sore, and I had claw marks on my neck and cheek. I couldn't stop grinning as I bounded up the steps to my home office.

I went through my action plan and the notes I had written down the evening before. Then looked up at the picture of my dad on the wall. He smiled down at me in black and white, and I smiled right back. I think I could see now through my tangled net of life experiences what he had tried to tell me years ago.

I wrote a simple email to Frank and copied it to compliance.

"*Dear Frank, I am writing to inform you of my resignation as of today. Thank you for the opportunities to grow and learn under your guidance. Please let me know how I can be of assistance during the transition period. I wish you and the company the very best going forward.*"

Almost immediately, my phone rang; it was Frank. He asked me what my action plan was for the week. I clicked on the 'send' button and said, "I think I'll go hiking with my dog."

He sounded a bit surprised. I told him about all the prospects that I had in my portfolio that I would like to give to one of his younger advisors. His choice. I would even spend time to make sure the transition would be successful. I wanted to make someone happy, to give them a fighting start. He hesitated but told me he understood; things could and would be rectified, it was sure. I told him I had made up my mind but would be available from this day forward. And when all this was over, he should come to Nashville, and I would buy him a beer. He told me he would like that.

When I hung up the phone, I made one more call, "Mr. Middleton!"

He was as boisterous as ever, "Hey, Banker! I was just thinking about you. Ready to make the transfer?"

I smiled, "Things have changed, Fred. There were complications, and we had to shut your account down. You'll have to wait a bit until the property closes. Shouldn't take too much more time; just let Linda know when you've closed. The person you deal with will be younger, smarter, and probably a whole lot prettier. I've decided to accept another opportunity. I hope you understand."

I told him about how he would benefit by dealing with the firm in a more permanent way. I would introduce him to the next advisor who would be more capable of helping him with his transaction and assured him that he was in good hands.

Fred busted out his words, "Bull-*loney*, Banker! What is really going on?"

I hesitated, glanced over to my dad's picture, and came clean, "I screwed up, Fred. I was so greedy that I put your cart of money before the horse. I knew when your mortgage hadn't closed that the transfer of your nest egg was not legal until you had a U.S. address. I thought that the house would close, and no one would be the wiser. I'm sorry. I let you down. I'm gonna quit this business. It's too dangerous for me. I'd rather trust myself around the snakes and wolves that I can see."

"All that then?" he said. "Anything I can do?"

"Yeah," I answered. "You might put a good word in for me."

"No problem, banker," he said. "You're the most honest 'suit' I ever met."

We both fell silent for a moment.

Then he asked me one last thing. "There's something I want to know. Did you really lose an engine in that puddle jumper?"

"Yeah." I paused.

My mind went to that dark night back in the summer of 1999.

I told him, "I was over Muscle Shoals heading south to Mississippi when I heard the engine quit. I managed to get it started again and gained as much altitude as I could. That gave me enough time to fish the plane's manual out of the glove box, turn on the cockpit lamp and begin reading. The problem was in the magnetos. The plane had two mags, and both were probably fouled. I found by leaning the mixture, I could get the engine hot enough to burn the muck off and keep it sputtering along to stay airborne till I could find a place to land. I had to watch the oil temp not to get too hot, or it would have quit for good. It was a lot of nervous work. You can turn runway lights on small airports by clicking your mic on Unicom frequencies, and I kept clicking on every one in range of a dead stick landing. I had a good flight instructor, Fred. He told me once that I would never be alone. Before the end of that night, I think I had turned on every runway light from Muscle Shoals to Biloxi."

He quietly replied, "So, you made it home OK?"

"Yeah," I stammered, "I did, and I think I've been turning runway lights on ever since."

We paused for a few more seconds.

Fred broke in, "Say, when I get to Nashville, I wanna take you to your favorite watering hole and catch up."

"Can't do it, Fred. We're not allowed back into that place. We'll have to find another bar."

He roared with laughter, "Goodbye, banker."

Goodbye, Fred. I hung up the phone and turned off the computer. I had a headache that was throbbing. For a couple minutes, I just stared at my reflection on the blank screen. The last time I had left my career, I had a plan. This time nothing. I had just basically retired again with no promise of an income. No map. And I was in the middle of a pandemic of epic proportion. The trail ahead was not marked with blazes.

I gazed at the numerous photos I'd taken of Zeke over the past four years on my desk. Those photographs were more than just a history of our trails and trials; they also provided me with a little bit of pride at how far I had come as an amateur photographer, something I had always tinkered with but never really had the time to do.

It was getting to be midmorning, and Zeke lay on his side at my feet, covering most of the floor in my small office. He looked up at me with questioning eyes.

"It's just you and me now, boy," I whispered to him.

He tilted his head to a forty-five and tried his best to understand. It occurred to me that he truly was the only other soul that shared my consternation. He remained silent and tacit, but by his continued stare, it was obvious that he sensed that things were rapidly changing in his world and in mine. Still wild within, with memories of a neglected youth tamed only by my constant companionship, Zeke had become as loyal as a dog could be. We had trusted each other with our lives, and I do not think he had ever experienced that trust with another human, or animal for that matter.

THE FOLLOWING MORNING, we got up early. This time I had my iPhone with me as we parked the car in the middle of downtown. The first picture I took of Zeke was at sunrise on a bridge that overlooked the entirety of a deserted bleak maze of buildings in the background. Zeke had his head turned to me, with a bright yellow-gold plume of sun rising against a blue skyline behind him.

The next picture I took was on Broadway. Zeke sat in the spot where just the year prior had been filled with a half-million football fans. He looked defiantly up the facing street as the traffic light above went from red to green. The bar lights were still brightly lit with no patrons inside.

We walked past hotels, restaurants, arcades. We went to the large legislative plaza where I used his trail commands to "sit" and "stay" and then walked back ten feet, fifty feet, a hundred feet, while he posed, still as a statue, waiting for his next instruction.

I took unbelievable photos as he sat motionless by iconic scenes without a passerby. We both felt comfortable in this environment; there was an eerie beauty to it, as if we were the last of humanity. I brought our lunch, and we sat and ate it in the middle of a silent six-lane avenue while traffic lights clicked above our heads.

We then walked to the Gulch, a young hip area of Nashville filled with upscale restaurants and modern condos with bamboo flooring and mid-century style lobbies. I took his picture beneath a painted mural of angel wings that were normally accessible only after an hour wait behind a line of tourists. We spent a full day hiking through the city where I had grown up, now almost unrecognizable. I saw the city as it truly was. Empty and artificial. It revealed itself through dirty alleys, large, expensive lobbies, and flashing neon lust. Still my city, still beautiful even with its weekend hordes of bridesmaids and stag parties. I think Zeke saw it as he did a blue-blazed trail and patiently waited for me at the forks. All of this had happened without a leash. We had graduated from that.

The next day I took Zeke to the largest museum in town, The Frist; it is full of both classic and ancient artworks housed in a stout and handsome grey stone building. There were no cars in the parking lot, nobody waiting in line to get in. I sat him on the steps as it started to rain and told him to stay. I walked the length of a football field away and turned around. He was barely a speck and had become a part of the chiseled architecture against a grey sky. I snapped the picture, then walked back and sat beside him in the slow drizzle. We both peered around our wet environment with the same tranquil expression. We were equal participants in a mystifying play in which we were the only actors, no audience to judge our performance.

Driving home, my mind refused to wander to any thought of the future. Zeke and I were silent the rest of the way, and at home, I downloaded our handy work and edited the photographs.

The following week we went hiking in other parts of the city and surrounding areas. Shopping malls, factories, sporting arenas. It was all the same. Devoid, depleted, evacuated, forsaken. I racked up a whole album of pictures that could fill a coffee table book. I never encountered another photographer, which surprised me. The empty city was a rare, life-changing photo op.

I got up one morning and sipped a cup of coffee. I left the phone on the counter, walked past the kitchen, and eyed the back door. I had grinned long ago about letting a dog exit that door, hoping he would disappear through the fence. Now he was staring at me in the living room where we had fought for the bread. All I had to do was mouth the words "Go," and that is all it took for Zeke to bound up and regain his four legs with immediate confidence. He shook his now 110-pound frame from nose to tail and made for the front door.

The sun was at near mid-sky and the neighborhood was empty, quiet. I left the house, letting Zeke take the lead today. He'd earned it being as patient as he had been all the days I had posed him this way and that.

I spotted another soul on the street approaching us. He was wearing a protective mask to shield him from the unknown virus that traveled so efficiently from human to human. I pulled my bandanna over my face and nodded to him. The man crossed to the other side of the street, passing us at a safe distance. Zeke trotted on disinterested, leading me to a destination that only he knew.

An hour later, we were crossing another six-lane, usually busy and bustling with road rage; this trek would have been impassable three months prior, but today it was a barren road. We both looked right, then left, and trod forward. We were now somewhere north of the city where I'd been by car but never by foot. Large graffiti covered the walls of dilapidated buildings with windows and doors protected by rusted iron bars.

By myself, I would have been petrified, but with the current state of affairs, I mustered no fear and having a bodyguard in the form of half dog half bear I would have welcomed the sight of another human. Zeke was in control now, dragging me to what he apparently wanted me to see. My city frozen in time with all its ugliness and filth; however, it was beautiful in a dog's eyes, a cornucopia of interesting smells.

Zeke had been bred and educated by this. The bankruptcy of human involvement, comfortable in his neglect and tutelage of abandonment. He neither expected a handout nor wanted it but had lived the first year of his life by scavenging and warring. It was the way he had survived. Only by cunning and combat had he made it through his first year, one that I will never fully know the extent of, his neglect and dereliction just footnotes on his shelter paperwork. Mine was the only forgiving hand that he had snapped and still retained access to, and loyal he was to that hand, for as great as that sin had been, my hand had caressed him in its aftermath with kindness and love, and he had given himself to me.

We encountered only one other human that day, a large disheveled gruff who advanced me from behind a stranded vehicle by a deserted storefront. He came at me with a drunken swagger, swearing belligerently, only to lay eyes on Zeke, who emerged quickly from my flank.

Zeke growled low at him as the hair on his back bristled in a black row. He grinned his teeth and wagged his tail in the same posture I had come to learn did not bode well to its intended. I smiled as the gruff stumbled off down the dirty sidewalk, finally cursing a slurring retort over his shoulder after gaining safe distance from us.

Zeke and I continued to inspect the slum-like streets with great curiosity. Block by block, we explored the gang rival tags scribbled on walls and abutments, his nose always to the ground. Teamed with a newfound brashness, we hunted this end of the city like two feral pack dogs until finally, the sun was low in the sky, and we started back home with no thought of tomorrow and carried with us only the memory of new sights and smells.

I don't think I have complained much throughout my life, appreciating every curveball for its lesson. But I found myself committing the cardinal sin of confusing richness with wealth, happiness with joy. I'd come close to losing my bearings when I attempted to deceive in order to skirt the rules and enrich myself. Many years ago, when I was tempted to throw my clients' life savings into the markets of 9/11 amid the looming recession, I had refused and tossed away a career. When faced with a divorce, with two infant boys, I chose to help raise them at all costs. I am reaping the rewards of that. I could not have asked for any better father/ son relationship than I have with my grown sons. They both have well exceeded my expectations; the men they've become have been truly amazing to watch. I've seen many things, but none compared to my sons being born, or my dad quitting his job for me and my brother, or countless other treasures that I couldn't have purchased with all the money in the world.

I did not know what poor was. I voiced this last out loud while Zeke walked beside me, turning his head thrusting his nose high in the night air. He understood nothing of my soliloquy, but he enjoyed its tone. I think it had a calming effect on both of us.

I felt an inner peace. Not a temporary emotion, but instead a permanent joy of satisfaction that I had not felt since I had been a kid. I was going home.

CHAPTER 21
HALLOWED GROUND

IT IS QUIET in my two-story bungalow. As I sit at my computer, I glance around at all that I have. The furniture inside is largely antique, with most of the credit going to my mother, who was a collector with an eye for solid and sturdy, expertly crafted pieces. My house is small, with dark, narrow, planked, hardwood floors, cheery light-yellow walls, with room enough for the things that are special to me. Among the treasured gifts are a few priceless but now headless chess pieces tied together with ribbon, which rest on the white wooden mantle next to a small hand-made stuffed woolen figurine of Zeke, complete with his red backpacks, a Christmas present from a friend. Below the mantle, next to the hearth, sit the chewed-up ventless logs I could never find the heart to throw away.

Most of my mother's crystal is displayed behind lead paned windows inside her old corner writing desk; nestled inside are a treasured stack of Dad's letters to home from the war; he was just eighteen but held the world on his shoulders. More of mother's glassware is placed on a serving table by the window next to a near-perfect drawing of Zeke's likeness which stands prominently in the middle, a gift from Elsa, my new daughter-in-law from the Netherlands. A full-sized book of pictures of Zeke taken on the barren city streets of Nashville lies on the tiled coffee table, and across from it, his red electric collar, a souvenir of the past, hangs on the corner of the fireplace.

It is in the cool of October and raining a downpour outside. The leaves on the trees are starting to turn with their first hint of fall. The weather has discouraged the strollers and dog walkers, so my neighborhood lay silent under a grey, thundering sky.

My backyard is bordered by a white vinyl picket fence and is spacious for a small lot; aside from having a large magnolia tree with broad leaves and white blossoms growing in the near center of it, in the far-left corner stands a tiny cross that marks the final resting place of the last member of our family, a toy shih tzu named Theo. He had lived to fifteen and been a close friend of Girl, the original biter, who now lay in peace beside him. Another three feet to the left lays Hobo, a homeless cat I rescued from the forks of a tall hackberry tree beside the house. She had lived to see Anthony graduate from high school before we had to put her down. Next to her are the bones of Buck, my first dog. This is truly hallowed ground.

Alex married the girl of his dreams in early August; it was a beautiful but small wedding, and they now live nearby in the suburbs north of Nashville. They smile at me happily from a framed picture atop my piano.

I have found and secured a job at a bank that pays one-third of the salary I have been accustomed to, and I am happy. I greet people in the lobby and refer them to a financial advisor if they need help.

I spent the warm weeks of the summer trekking across newly opened state parks and getting lost therein with Zeke. Together, we have walked most of the North and South Rim of Savage Gulf. He now knows the Blue Blazes himself and leads me to his favorite bluffs, where we sit above the gorge and bask for hours. He no longer fears what is around the corner and swims with abandon in the deep river by the falls.

I am sitting in my office thinking about when I had first asked Alex why he had given me the large mongrel for Christmas. His short answer was that he thought I needed the exercise. Exercise indeed. Over the last three-year period, I calculated that we had walked over 1,800 miles, much of it over terrain I would have never agreed to had he not been pulling me at the end of his leash. I also calculated that I had spent hours, days, and weeks trying to think of how to get rid of this dog. I'd driven him more times than I can remember back to the shelter from which he came, only to sit in the parking lot telling him all the reasons I could not keep him, then starting the engine and driving home as he sat still in the back seat like a bad child. I had not wanted him and fought hard for reasons not to keep him. Zeke had not wanted me and had plotted for his freedom, escaping more times than I can recall.

Now we abide together, attached by the prehistoric bond that goes back to the dawn of the hunter-gatherers in the savanna where man and dog were created. We possess no common language other than the private memories and near-death experiences that we alone share, and aside from the leash, there is nothing physical that holds us together.

Sometime in the future, this old bungalow will be demolished, making room for new and fresh tall skinnies. My time here will be forgotten. They will find the bones in the mass cemetery in the backyard and likely call it in.

Zeke will turn thirty-five in dog years in December. I am sixty-four, so we will both turn seventy in the same year. If we are able, we will spend our final years together. When it gets difficult for him to walk, he will live on a blanket by the fireplace in the den, and often we will take joyrides with the windows all the way down so he can throw feeble insults at the squirrels. When he starts to lose his appetite, I will bake him fresh fish with a crusty bread coating, his favorite. When his life is over, I will take him to his final place, in the backyard, with the rest of the bones. I will promise him to live as he taught me, not in dread of what might be taken, but rather in awe of what has been given, exactly what my father had tried to teach me.

We are bound by love, nothing else.

Without the strength and goodness of my grandfather, the humor and wisdom of my dad, and the gentle, hardworking women who stood beside them and worked the land, I would have been poor.

Without Zeke, I may not have survived my fall from grace, and I certainly would have never realized that God lived so close to my house.

It is a tranquil moment, with him laying at my feet waiting for a hint that we might share another hill, and me about to write a book, not about cruises and the world adventure I had wished for, but about the realization of real wealth that I had found by having him.

I turn back to the keyboard of my computer and, with large and slightly clumsy man hands, hunt and peck the following words:

"It was the worst Christmas ever ..."

AUTHOR BIO

STEPHEN ELLIS HAMILTON is an avid hiker, a private pilot and a lover of dogs. He was born in Nashville and spent his summers growing up on the two farms of his grandfathers in West Tennessee. After earning a B.S. in Chemical Engineering, he spent thirty-four years as a Financial Advisor before turning to his love of the outdoors and writing. He wrote this book during the pandemic of 2020 as a memoir to document his feelings after he gave up a career to follow his dog. In his own words, “I received my finest wealth education alone, lost in the hills of East Tennessee, guided by the stars and the sun, with the love of a dog beside me and thirty-five pounds of all I needed on my back.”

OIL ON WATER PRESS

True-Life Stories and Memoir

oilonwaterpress.com

CPSIA information can be obtained
at www.ICGtesting.com
Printed in the USA
BVHW080823020922
646101BV00005B/21

9 781909 394872